BATTERSEA
HERE FOR EVERY DOG AND CAT

DOG
PUZZLE BOOK

BATTERSEA

HERE FOR EVERY DOG AND CAT

DOG

PUZZLE BOOK

MORE THAN 100 CANINE CONUNDRUMS

WELBECK

Published in 2022 by Welbeck
An Imprint of Welbeck Non-Fiction Limited,
part of Welbeck Publishing Group.
Based in London and Sydney.
www.welbeckpublishing.com

Produced under license from Battersea Dogs Home Ltd to go towards
supporting the work of Battersea Dogs & Cats Home (registered
charity no 206394). For all licensed products sold by Welbeck across
their Battersea range, Welbeck will donate a minimum of £10,000
plus VAT in royalties to Battersea Dogs Home Limited, which gives all
its profits to Battersea Dogs & Cats Home. Battersea.org.uk

All puzzles created by The Puzzle House except Multiple Chews,
created by Ian Greensill.

Copyright © Welbeck Non-Fiction Limited 2022

A CIP catalogue record for this book is available from the
British Library.

ISBN 978 1 80279 412 0
Printed in the UK.

10 9 8 7 6 5 4 3 2 1

MIX
Paper from
responsible sources
FSC® C171272

SUPPORTING THE · HERE FOR EVERY DOG & CAT · WORK OF BATTERSEA

Battersea is here for every dog and cat, and has been since 1860.

Battersea takes dogs and cats in, gives them the expert care they need and finds them new homes that are just right for them.

They help pet owners make informed choices, provide training advice, and campaign for changes in the law.

And they help other rescue centres and charities at home and abroad because they want to be here for every dog and cat, wherever they are, for as long as they need Battersea.

Your purchase will help Battersea continue its important work.

Thank you.

battersea.org.uk

Contents

PUZZLES

KEEP IN SHAPE

Solution on page 229.

Individual letters have been replaced by symbols. The first group stands for the letters L, E, A and D – making the word LEAD.

The symbols remain constant throughout all the groups.
What dog-related words do the other groups make?

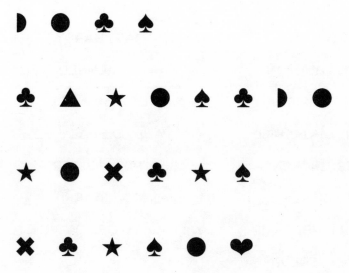

FAMOUS OWNERS

Solution on page 229.

Here's a list of famous folk who were all well known for their canine companions.

The names are hidden in the letter square. All words are in straight lines and can go horizontally, vertically and diagonally. They may read forwards or backwards.

EMILY   BRONTE

RICHARD   BURTON

AGATHA   CHRISTIE

WINSTON   CHURCHILL

CHARLES   DICKENS

WALT   DISNEY

QUEEN   ELIZABETH (II)

SIGMUND   FREUD

THOMAS   HARDY

JOHN F.   KENNEDY

MARILYN   MONROE

PAUL   O'GRADY

BEATRIX   POTTER

RINGO   STARR

WILLIAM   WORDSWORTH

```
W O R D S W O R T H N E R A C
M I G D A R N B S E L R A H C
R O N R Y N E O E U A C U P H
K J N S A A Y U T T H R E O R
E O L R T D Q L S R C V A T I
N L S R O O Y A I H U R H T S
N D I C K E N S I R E B T E C
E X P Z N Y T L O R A J A R O
D H R S A I L W D N U M G I S
Y L I A E B O A R R A C A B A
Q D O J R W E L F I A J N F M
U B G O S I L T L D Y H R P O
O X N H P A U L H I A E C E H
U T I N E M I L Y E U E Y I T
E A R F E W S A Y D R A H R R
```

CA-NINE

Solution on page 230.

Nine boxes. Nine different letters of the alphabet. Solve the cunning clues and write the letters in the appropriate spaces in the grid.

When all nine letters are in place, a word for a canine breed is created.

CLUES

1. Pursue, follow after   2   3   5   1   8

2. Move at speed   9   6   4

3. Clear an irritation from the nose.
   Bless you!   1   4   8   8   7   8

1	2	3	4	5	6	7	8	9

DOG BASKET

Solution on page 230.

The dogs need to go in their basket. In the letter box the word DOGS appears along with three other words of four letters. The words appear in straight lines of letters that can go across, back, up, down or diagonally.

Use these words to fill the empty basket by creating a word square in which the words read the same going across and down.

Z	D	O	G	S	E
W	L	I	W	W	G
G	U	O	Z	O	D
L	W	R	G	W	W
A	Y	A	H	O	V
D	T	W	U	Q	W

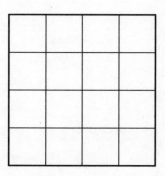

MATCH UP

Solution on page 230.

Four friends meet up to walk their dogs. From the remarks made and the information given, can you discover the names of the people (A to D) and match them to their dogs (1 to 4)?

Dog 1 has black ears, a black-and-white tail and a white collar.

Dog 2 has black ears, a white tail and a white collar.

Dog 3 has white ears, a black tail and a black collar.

Dog 4 has white ears, a white tail and a black collar. This is not the dog called Suzie.

Gentleman A says: "Alfie's dog is called Rover. Maya's dog isn't the one called Arnold."

Lady B says: "Lisa's dog has black ears but mine hasn't."

Lady C says: "My lovely dog Cooper hasn't got an all-white tail."

Gentleman D says: "My dog does not have a black collar but he does have the same tail colour as Theo's dog."

WORTH IT!

Solution on page 231.

What's a dog worth? They are all beyond price, of course. However, with these dogs we have taken the letters from their names and given them each a value. Six different letters in all are used.

The numbers allocated are between 1 and 6. The total of each name is worked out by adding individual letters together.

L E O = 6

B O B = 9

B E L L E = 14

B E L L A = 18

What is   M A B E L   worth?

QUIZ CROSSWORD

Solution on page 232.

Solve the answer to each question in order to complete the grid.

ACROSS

3. What word describes what you do when you put your dog's name down for a training class? (5)
7. The dog is said to be humankind's best what? (6)
8. If the A in RSPCA was just a single creature, what would A stand for? (6)
10. What name is given to an emotional film, such as *Marley and Me*, which often has a sad ending? (4.6)
11. What manner of walking is used for dogs in shows, but is more often used for horses? (4)
12. A lively dog is said to be full of what? (5)
13. Which film about a very large dog shares its name with a famous German composer? (9)
16. What is another word for cautious? (7)
21. What type of dog was 13 Across? (2.7)
22. What means 'of great worth' either in terms of money or importance? (5)
23. What standard on a pole can be used as a marker on a course? (4)
24. Which racing dogs hunt by sight rather than scent? (10)
26. What is also known as the gazelle hound? (6)
27. What is another name for a field, where a sheepdog works? (6)
29. How many colours are there in a tricolour dog? (5)

DOWN

1. Whose job is it to generate the production of litters of puppies? (7)
2. Which sense is linked to listening? (7)
3. What is the perimeter of a field sometimes called? (4)
4. What name is given to a wild creature's den? (4)
5. Books about dogs which are not necessarily fact are called what? (7)
6. Which dog, originally from central Asia, has accompanied Arctic explorers on their expeditions? (7)
9. Which native of the Hebrides has been popular with English and Scottish royal families? (4.7)
14. What sound is made when a tail hits the ground sharply? (4)
15. A bark can be used to do what, in addition to expressing pleasure? (4)
17. What nationality is the Spinone? (7)
18. Where does the Groenendael originally come from? (7)
19. Which History Museum in London has exhibits about creatures and their world? (7)
20. Which word describes exercises and activities in the open air? (7)
24. What is an alternative name for movement as in 11 Across? (4)
25. What follows 're-' to mean how a dog is found a new place to live and a new family? (4)

ROUND THE BLOCK

Solution on page 232.

Many dog owners take their pet 'round the block' for a walk. In this puzzle each answer has eight letters. Write the answer words in the grid, with each first letter going in a numbered square. Then you have to decide whether to go round the block in a clockwise or anti-clockwise direction. All the answers have to interlock together.

CLUES

1. Regular physical activity

2. Absorbed food

3. Big name on the big screen. Rin-Tin-Tin was one of the first! (4,4)

4. Dog's overseas travel document

5. Breed of cocker spaniel from across the pond

6. Affectionately

7. Gundog which shares its name with a northern French province

8. A time-keeping canine?

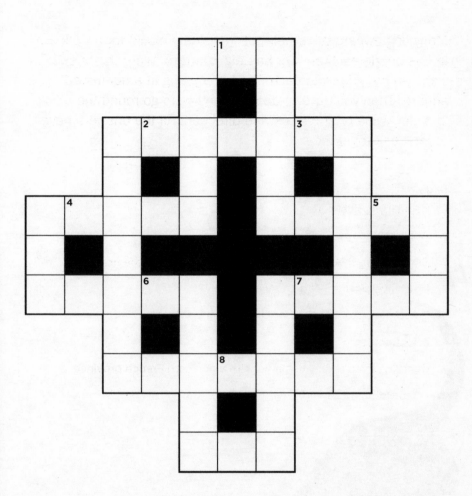

WHAT AM I?

Solution on page 233.

Use all the clues
And give it a try,
Work out the answer,
And say what am I.

My first is in CARE
And also in CALL.

My second is in BOWL
But isn't in BALL.

My third is in GROWL
And also in BARK.

My fourth is in GUARD
But isn't in DARK.

My fifth is in TAIL
And also in SIGH.

SIX FIX

Solution on page 233.

All answers have six letters and fit into the grid reading in a clockwise direction. We give you the starting point for the answer to Clue 1, but after that you have to work out in which hexagonal cell the answer begins.

CLUES

1. Hound with brown coat and short hair

2. Outside area of a house with play area

3. Dog house!

4. Humbly, submissively

5. Fully grown

6. Set walkways, paths

7. Tasty piece of food

8. Farm animals

9. Small

10. Walk too slowly

11. Moved its tail from side to side

12. Asked for food

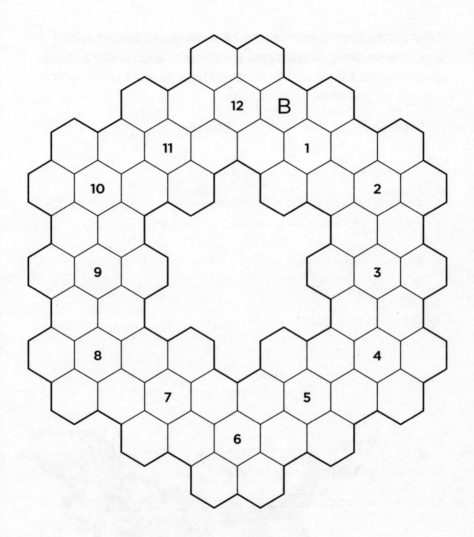

SHADY SEVENS

Solution on page 233.

Place all the listed seven-letter words to read across the grid in such an order that the diagonal line of letters in the shaded seven spaces forms the name of a breed of dog.

OUTDOOR

PUPPIES

RUNNING

SHIH-TZU

SPANIEL

STRETCH

WORKING

SIRIUS

Solution on page 233.

All our dogs are stars in their own way. Sirius is known as the Dog Star and it's the brightest light in the night sky. Solve the canine clues, which are listed at random.

Each five-letter answer starts in a space with an odd number (1, 3, 5, 7, 9 and 11) and ends in a space with an even number (2, 4, 6, 8, 10 and 12).

The letter in space 1 is A.

CLUES

Not moving

A nose

A special reward

Watchful, attentive

Pursues, stalks

This goes before Bernard in the name of a breed

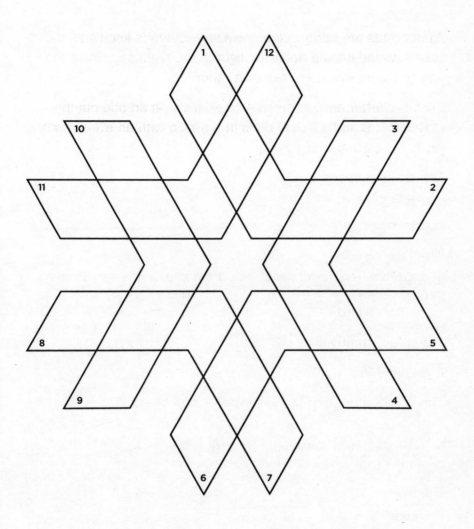

MULTIPLE CHEWS

Solution on page 234.

Chew on these multiple choice quiz questions, based on well-known television dogs.

1. In the long-running sitcom *Frasier*, what was the name of the energetic Jack Russell terrier owned by Frasier's father?

   A Kelsey

   B Eric

   c Eddie

   D Connor

2. In *Coronation Street*, what was the name of Chesney Brown's Great Dane?

   A Becks

   B Keano

   c Schmeichel

   D Scholesy

3. In the 1960s TV series *The Beverly Hillbillies*, what was the name of their bloodhound?

   A Baron

   B Count

   c Duke

   D Earl

4. In *The Wonder Years*, which ran from 1988 to 1993, what was the name of Kevin's dog?

A Buddy

B Buster

C Nipper

D Sonny

5. In *The Muppet Show*, Rowlf the Dog predominantly played which instrument?

A Banjo

B Drums

C Piano

D Saxophone

6. What was the name of Ethel's dog in *EastEnders*, an apricot-coloured standard poodle who appeared in the very first episode in 1985 and was in the show until 1993?

A Rocky

B Roly

C Rory

D Roxy

7. In the US TV series *Hart to Hart*, which ran from 1979 to 1984, what was the name of the pet dog of the butler, Max?

A Frankie

B Freddie

c Freeway

D Frodo

8. In *The Big Bang Theory*, what was the name of Raj's pet Yorkshire terrier, given to him by Howard and Bernadette?

A Basil

B Cinnamon

c Ginger

D Saffron

9. In *Doctor Who*, what was the name of the robot dog that appeared periodically over the years?

A K7

B K8

c K9

D K10

10. In the US TV series *The Dukes of Hazzard*, which ran from 1979 to 1985, what was the name of the slow-paced basset hound owned by Sheriff Rosco Coltrane?

A Blaze

B Flash

C Lightning

D Thunder

11. In *Columbo*, what was the rather unimaginative name he gave to his basset hound?

A Dog

B Fido

C Mutt

D You

12. In *Downton Abbey*, the Earl of Grantham's yellow Labrador retriever had the name of which goddess?

A Hera

B Iris

C Isis

D Juno

THAT'S MY DOG

Solution on page 234.

There is no doubting the breed of dog this owner has. Rearrange all the letters in the personal name to form the name of the type of dog.

R O G E R   D E T R E L V I N E

CLUE:
Two words

THREE FRIENDS

Solution on page 234.

Can you match the dogs to their owners and coat colours?

Luna, George and Winston are three friendly dogs that live in the same street.

One dog is black, one is grey and one is white. Oddly enough, the three owners are Mr Black, Ms Grey and Mr White.

No dog has a coat colouring that matches their owner's name. No dog has a coat colouring with the same initial letter as their own name.

Luna is owned by one of the gentlemen.

WALKIES

Solution on page 235.

A classic quick crossword with dog-themed clues.

ACROSS

8. Well being (7)
9. A canine or a mound of rough stones (5)
10. Makes progress (5)
11. Normal, characteristic (7)
12. Look after (4)
13. Being idle (8)
16. Playfulness (8)
18. Second hand (4)
21. Try (7)
23. Pals (5)
25. Dig deeply (5)
26. Disobedient (7)

DOWN

1. Travel through water (4)
2. Intelligent (6)
3. Boggy area (5)
4. Slender (4)
5. Canine from north of the border (7)
6. Ferocious (6)
7. Fenced in (8)
12. Gives orders (8)
14. Grow older (3)
15. Walloped the tail hard on the ground (7)
17. Calm down (6)
19. Looked for (6)
20. Rough land (5)
22. Very small (4)
24. Sounds like you look upwards to see this terrier (4)

DOG COLLAR

Solution on page 235.

Solve the clues, which are in no particular order, and slot the seven-letter answers back into their correct places in the dog collar. The last letter of one answer is also the first letter of the next.

Answer 1 begins with a letter E.

CLUES

Made haste

Remain after experiencing great hardship and difficulty

Canine meals

Old sheepdog's nationality

Utterly dedicated to its owner

E

FITTING IN

Solution on page 236.

We all hope that a newcomer to the home will fit in as one of the family. In this puzzle a word with a canine connection has to be fitted in to the spaces so that the word becomes complete.

All the words in 1 need the same three-letter word, and a similar pattern follows for 2 and 3. Three different words for three different sections.

1. S _ _ _ G E R E D

   S _ _ _ E C O A C H

   _ _ _ I N E

2. O C _ _ _ R E N C E

   _ _ _ T A I N S

   S _ _ _ V Y

3. C A R _ _ _

   _ _ _ U L A N T

   C O M _ _ _ E

CROSS BREEDS

Solution on page 236.

The letters in SEVEN words linked to the canine world have been rearranged in alphabetical order.

Can you put the letters back in their correct order and slot them in the grid so that 4 across and the centre column reading down will spell out the names of two breeds of dog?

1. A C D M M N O

2. A D E R R S W

3. D E E I L S Y

4. E E R S S T T

5. D E F I N R S

6. B D E H R S U

7. C E E L T S S

SIXTH SENSE

Solution on page 236.

Does a dog have a sixth sense, an ability to make something out that humans are unable to? With this puzzle it's not what you see that matters, it's what you cannot see! There's a jumble of letters of the alphabet in the box.

What you need to find are the letters that do not appear. There are SIX of them. Use each missing letter once only to make a word that describes a dog.

Y B O Z M
G Q
H C J
L
W K A
T
V X S U
P

MULTIPLE CHEWS

Solution on page 236.

Chew on these multiple choice quiz questions based on dogs in classic films.

1. 1939: In the film *The Wizard of Oz*, what was the name of Dorothy's dog?

   A Lilo
   B Rolo
   c Toby
   D Toto

2. 1955: In the film *The Lady and the Tramp*, what breed of dog was Lady?

   A American cocker spaniel
   B English cocker spaniel
   c English springer spaniel
   D King Charles spaniel

3. 1973: In *The Biggest Dog in the World*, what was the name of the titular sheepdog in the film?

   A Digby
   B Digsby
   c Rigby
   D Rigsby

4. 1975: What was the name of the film starring Al Pacino and John Cazale about a Brooklyn bank robbery and hostage situation that went wrong?

A   Dog Day Afternoon

B   Dog Soldiers

C   Reservoir Dogs

D   The Dogs of War

5. 1985: In *Back to the Future*, what was the name of Doc Brown's sheepdog?

A   Darwin

B   Einstein

C   Faraday

D   Newton

6. 1989: Who was the eponymous Dogue De Bordeaux 'cop buddy' to police investigator (Scott) Turner, played by Tom Hanks?

A   Hooch

B   Mooch

C   Pooch

D   Scooch

7. 1989: In *Honey, I Shrunk the Kids*, what was the name of the Szalinski family's pet Russell Terrier?

A Hadron

B Neutron

c Proton

D Quark

8. 1989: What was the name of the first Wallace & Gromit film?

A *A Close Shave*

B *A Grand Day Out*

c *A Matter of Loaf and Death*

D *The Wrong Trousers*

9. 1992: What film, which spawned a series of sequels and spin-offs, starred a St Bernard dog named after a famous classical composer?

A Bach

B Beethoven

c Handel

D Mozart

10. 1993: In *Homeward Bound: The Incredible Journey*, the story of two dogs and a cat getting lost in the mountains, what breed of dog was Shadow?

A American bulldog

B Bernese mountain dog

c Golden retriever

D Labrador

11. 1993: In Tim Burton's *The Nightmare Before Christmas*, what was the name of Jack's 'ghost dog' with a glowing nose?

A Aero

B Hero

c Nero

D Zero

12. 1994: In *The Mask*, what was the name of the pet dog of the main character, Stanley Ipkiss, played by Jim Carrey?

A Halo

B Milo

c Polo

D Solo

A TO Z

Solution on page 237.

Here's an A to Z of dog-related words (minus an X!). The words are hidden in the letter square. All words are in straight lines and can go horizontally, vertically and diagonally. They may read forwards or backwards.

There is one word that appears three times. Can you sniff it out?

ADOPT	JOY	STROLL
BALL	KNOWING	TRUE
COAT	LIVELY	UNIQUE
DAWDLE	MISCHIEF	VITAL
EAGER	NEAT	WELL BEHAVED
FEARLESS	OWNER	YAWN
GOOD NATURED	PRAISE	ZOOM
HEROIC	QUIET	
IDEAL	RECREATION	

```
T  U  L  P  T  D  B  F  O  L  L  O  W  Y  L
A  G  Z  P  A  O  E  A  L  Z  D  J  L  V  L
E  U  O  W  T  I  Z  O  L  U  E  E  I  G  O
N  D  D  O  H  V  R  Q  Z  L  V  T  Y  A  R
A  L  R  C  D  T  Z  U  L  I  A  J  O  Y  T
E  D  S  X  S  N  R  I  L  L  H  E  M  P  S
P  I  N  O  I  T  A  E  R  C  E  R  B  R  C
M  U  P  K  E  S  R  T  O  R  B  B  U  I  W
O  N  H  R  N  A  Y  A  U  Y  L  D  O  V  L
G  I  L  O  A  O  T  O  F  R  L  R  C  A  B
A  Q  Z  L  D  I  W  E  D  F  E  M  E  E  J
N  U  O  B  O  N  S  I  L  H  W  D  Y  A  O
P  E  O  N  E  R  G  E  N  O  I  A  C  G  E
Q  U  M  R  E  L  T  S  Z  G  W  E  B  E  Y
F  E  A  R  L  E  S  S  A  N  U  E  U  R  T
```

POINTER

Solution on page 238.

Each answer contains FOUR letters. The first letter goes in a numbered triangle, the second letter directly above it, the third letter to the right and the fourth to the left.

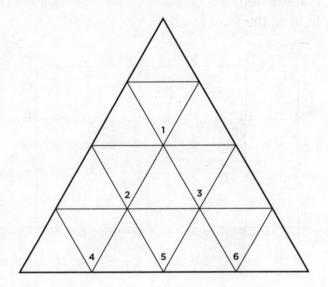

CLUES

1. 2009 movie with Richard Gere, *A Dog's* _____

2. Protein part of a dog's diet

3. An appeal, which a dog achieves without speaking!

4. Instruction to not move

5. Festival event

6. Another instruction to come to the person issuing the command

GIVE ME FIVE!

Solution on page 238.

Solve the canine clues, which are listed at random. All the answers contain five letters. You have to fit the answers back in the frame, going either across or down.

There is a starter letter to help you on the way. There is only one way to fit all the words back.

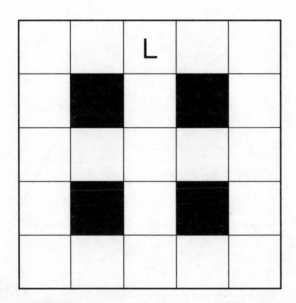

CLUES

Acquire knowledge

Toboggans pulled by dogs

A winner!

Astound with agility

Gasps, breathes heavily

Shouts for a dog to come to heel

DOG TAGS

Solution on page 238.

The letters on the dog tags can be rearranged to form words. There are letters on individual tags, shared letters between two tags, and the space in the middle needs to be filled by a letter that is in all three tags.

You are looking for the names of three different dog markings.

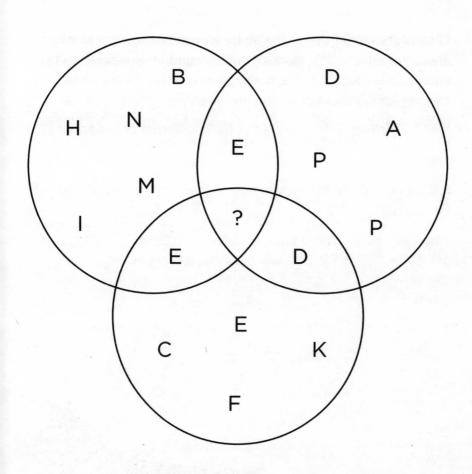

WELL BRED

Solution on page 239.

Each of the 26 letters of the alphabet has been replaced by a number from 1 to 26. Work out which number represents which letter to complete the crossword-style grid, which has words reading across and down. You are given the letters in the word BRED to start you off. 1 = B, 2 = R, 3 = E, 4 = D. Straight away you can fill in all the squares that contain the numbers 1, 2, 3 and 4.

Fill in the 1 to 26 grid with letters of the alphabet as you work them out.

When you have worked out the code, the letters 9, 11, 11, 3, 8, 19, 10, 8, 5, 16, 22, 3, 2 will spell out a breed of dog.

9	11	11	3	8	19	10	8	5	16	22	3	2

Grid (codeword puzzle):

	22		16		6				23		16		1	
8	9	6	17	2	9	13		5	9	20	7	15	3	4
	10		4		10		5		21		20		9	
1	2	3	4		13	10	14	3	5		19	17	12	5
			13		5		15				3		13	
18	17	10	3	6		2	3	4	5	3	6	6	3	2
	5		4		1		6		10		3			
19	3	6		2	7	5	3	6	6	3		1	7	25
			11		2		2		5		20		21	
5	6	1	3	2	8	9	2	4		15	9	21	8	5
	9		3				10		5		20			
9	12	3	4		21	22	3	13	19		20	7	24	3
	12		10		9		2		10		9		3	
14	3	8	8	3	13	5		17	6	10	13	10	6	15
	4		12		14			26		5		5		

1	2	3	4	5	6	7	8	9	10	11	12	13
14	15	16	17	18	19	20	21	22	23	24	25	26

SHADOW PLAY

Solution on page 239.

Answer the questions going across in the top grid. All answers have seven letters. When the top grid is complete, take the letters in the shaded squares and place them vertically, one below the other, in the lower grid.

When you have completed the lower grid, a famous proverb with a canine connection will be revealed.

CLUES

1. A dog will do this when cleaning or rubbing with its tongue

2. Protected, shielded

3. Caressed a dog along the direction of its coat

4. Resting, not standing

5. King who gave his name to a breed of spaniel

6. A cross breed

7. Providing with food

8. A hobby or leisure activity

9. Assessed how heavy a dog is

10. A glum expression, but maybe a canine is not to blame!

1							
2							
3							
4							
5							
6							
7							
8							
9							
10							

1	2	3	4	5	6	7	8	9	10

THAT'S MY DOG

Solution on page 239.

There is no doubting the breed of dog this owner has. Rearrange all the letters in the personal name to form the name of the type of dog.

D A N   G E E T A R

CLUE:

Two words

BEST FOOT FORWARD

Solution on page 240.

Set off on your daily constitutional with your best friend and move forward with this puzzle. There are two clues each time and two solutions.

The first clue is general, the second has a canine link. The solutions are almost the same, the only difference being that in the second word the middle letter has moved forward in the alphabet.

1. Wine barrel * Animal clinician
   (both words have three letters)

2. Sparse, inadequate * Smell which provides a trail
   (both words have five letters)

3. Setting, arranging * Having fun with a game
   (both words have seven letters)

4. Corroborated * Followed the rules, obeyed
   (both words have nine letters)

SIX FIX

Solution on page 240.

All answers have six letters and fit into the grid reading in a clockwise direction. We give you the starting point for the answer to Clue 1, but after that you have to work out in which hexagonal cell the answer begins.

CLUES

1. Breed also known as the Persian Greyhound

2. Helpful, beneficial

3. The dam is the _____ parent of puppies

4. Canine you can sit on your knee

5. Colour, such as a retriever

6. Greatly loved

7. Describes a thin country path

8. Required, needed

9. Large groups of people

10. Shape of a ring or loop

11. Information poster announcing where a footpath is, for example

12. Sight

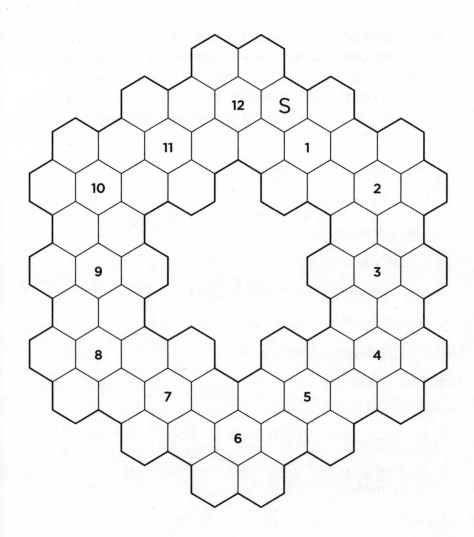

ROUND THE BLOCK

Solution on page 240.

Many dog owners take their pet 'round the block' for a walk. In this puzzle each answer has eight letters. Write the answer words in the grid, with each first letter going in a numbered square. Then you have to decide whether to go round the block in a clockwise or anti-clockwise direction. All the answers have to interlock together.

CLUES

1. Small, Welsh dog with a white coat, named after the house where it was first bred

2. Country walkway

3. You might hear a bark when this rings

4. Warm reddish-brown colour of a canine's coat

5. _____ King Charles Spaniel

6. French breed, the Pyrenean _____dog, called the Patou at home

7. Armed services, who use retrievers and German shepherds in their work

8. Nationality of the Inuit dog

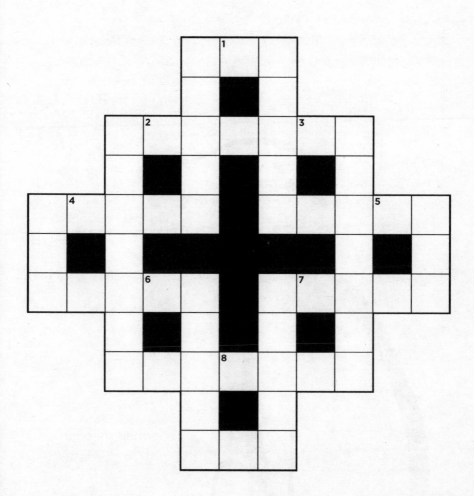

TURN AROUND

Solution on page 240.

Some dogs will turn around three times before settling and lying down for a well-earned rest. In each of the sentences below, there are three words which are made up of the same letters.

They are anagrams of each other. Can you turn the letters around and work out what they are? A well-earned rest awaits at the end!

1. We have a very large dog, which is generally very well behaved. It is quite a dignified creature with a regal bearing. He loves music, especially English music, and his favourite composer is Edward Elgar.

2. Ernest (known to all as Ernie) enters the room looking for his dog Eric. Eric is nowhere to be found and Ernie is beginning to resent the fact the others think he has lost him.

3. Grannie is nearing the ripe old age of eighty and her elderly dog Ranger is also earning himself a bit of a reputation as a grandee of the canine world.

CANINE CODES

Solution on page 241.

Answer the questions across in the upper grid. All answers have eight letters, except for Clue 2, which has two words of four letters.

Take the key-coded letters and place them in the lower grid to provide you with a famous saying. Column H reading down will reveal some impressive dogs.

CLUES

1. Going and returning with something which has been thrown

2. A coat which is not short and trim, like that of Clue 9 (4.4)

3. The hearth, where dog and owner might sit in the evening

4. Take this if it is wet on a daily walk

5. The most recently born in a litter

6. Drew, made a pencil drawing

7. A wide open view, a vista

8. Attachment and loyalty from owner to dog and vice versa

9. Short-legged breed of dog originally from China

10. Look in this direction to focus on the Dog Star

	A	B	C	D	E	F	G	H
1								
2								
3								
4								
5								
6								
7								
8								
9								
10								

D10	E2	A5		B6	B1	D3	A7		F7		
A8	B2	E5		E10	G1	G3		C4	B7	C3	C9
C10	B5	A4	E7	E3	C6	A2	A1				

K9

Solution on page 241.

A 9 x 9 crossword with a cryptic twist.

ACROSS

3. Animals moved by dogs formed by hydrogen seep (5)
6. Remains of broken chairs found covering a dog (4)
7. Weeps uncontrollably cleaning kennels (5)
8. Last ailment reveals part of the body (4)
10. Eats well on things found in estuaries (5)
14. Outdoor receiver used for serving a meal (4)
15. Projections of a comb give bite (5)
16. Sounds like an Italian farewell to this dog (4)
17. I leave RNLI as arranged with angry growl (5)

DOWN

1. I'm dreaming of this type of Christmas dog colour (5)
2. Return of badly lit information technology lacking courage (5)
4. We hold together dog that bayed (6)
5. Holes in needles give animals vision (4)
9. Pups? That's rubbish! (6)
11. Sounds like a building plot linked to 5 DOWN (5)
12. Reveals dogs have got talent performances? (5)
13. Underfed animal discovered little and thin (4)

TURN AROUND

Solution on page 242.

Some dogs will turn around three times before settling and lying down for a well-earned rest. In each of the sentences below, there are three words which are made up of the same letters.

They are anagrams of each other. Can you turn the letters around and work out what they are? A well-earned rest awaits at the end!

1. Thomas and Geraldine run a dog rehoming centre in Dorset. All the food for the animals is stored in a barn on site. When the dogs first arrive, they are sorted into areas according to their size and age.

2. The dogs live in small chalets. Geraldine carries a satchel with her at all times with the animals' details recorded there. The latches on the doors are specially made to ensure all the inhabitants are safe and secure.

3. Alerting all the carers at the centre is an integral part of the security system there. In case of fire there is a grassy outdoor area in the shape of a triangle where all must meet for a roll call.

ABOUT BREEDING

Solution on page 242.

The names of breeds of dog have been divided into a line
of letters. Can you work out the names of the two breeds in
each case? Lines 1 and 2 contain two breeds of five letters;
in 3 there are two seven-letter names. The letters read in
chronological order.

1. C O H O U R G I N D

2. D I S P N I G T Z O

3. S W H A M I O P Y E P E D T

MULTIPLE CHEWS

Solution on page 242.

Chew on these multiple choice quiz questions. Dogs come in all shapes and sizes, but these questions are based on specific breeds.

1. What breed of dog is known for having a bluish-black tongue?

   A Lhasa Apso

   B Chow Chow

   c Afghan Hound

   D American bulldog

2. What breed of dog was Wellard, who belonged to Robbie Jackson (played by Dean Gaffney) in *EastEnders*?

   A Belgian Tervuren

   B German shepherd

   c Portuguese water dog

   D Rhodesian ridgeback

3. What breed of dog, which originated in central Africa, does not bark but instead emits a kind of yodelling cry?

   A Basenji

   B Borzoi

   c Saluki

   D Samoyed

4. The Lhasa Apso originated in which country?

A China

B Japan

C Nepal

D Tibet

5. Which terrier is named after a mining town in the north-east of England and is said to have a similar look to a lamb?

A Bedlington terrier

B Cowley terrier

C Dandie Dinmont terrier

D Sealyham terrier

6. The Jack Russell terrier was named after a 'sporting parson' from which English county?

A Cornwall

B Devon

C Dorset

D Somerset

7. Bo, a gift to the family of President Barack Obama in 2009, was what breed of dog?

A Bearded collie
B Old English sheepdog
C Poodle
D Portuguese water dog

8. The Cane Corso originated in which country?

A France
B Italy
C Portugal
D Spain

8. The Dandie Dinmont terrier is named after a character in the 1815 novel *Guy Mannering* by which author?

A Emily Brontë
B Jane Austen
C Lord Byron
D Sir Walter Scott

10. Which dog is alternatively known as the Persian greyhound?

A Basenji

B Borzoi

c Saluki

D Samoyed

11. When Dalmatians are born, what colour are their spots?

A Black

B Brown

c Pink

D They don't have any

12. The Great Dane originated in which country?

A Denmark

B Germany

c Hungary

D Netherlands

QUIZ CROSSWORD

Solution on page 243.

Solve the answer to each question in order to complete the grid.

ACROSS

3. What word describes a metal disc, usually with an inscription, to commemorate success in a show or competition event? (5)
7. Which name is given to a beer and lemonade mixture that is also a popular female dog name, especially in Ireland? (6)
8. What's the term for the fold of skin that protects a dog's organ of sight? (6)
10. Which large dog with a good sense of smell is used to hunt things? (10)
11. Which mythological figure became popular as a dog name after the *Thor* movies and *The Avengers* franchise? (4)
12. What's the name for a daily journal logging notes about your pet? (5)
13. What name is given to the bony frameworks of dogs and of humans? (9)

16. Where does Gromit the dog travel on Wallace's motorbike? (7)
21. Which gun dog has a name suggesting they save every situation? (9)
22. What can be dog walking areas and ways of getting around a garden? (5)
23. Which word goes before Of Dogs, in a River Thames setting? (4)
24. What was the profession of Alex Graham, who created Fred Basset? (10)
26. What breed of dog can be standard, miniature or toy? (6)
27. What type of sharp point is used to give dogs medical injections? (6)
29. Which word means a dog stays where it is told? (5)

DOWN

1. Which word is short for a Shetland sheepdog? (7)
2. Which word describes the area inside the home of a dog and owner? (7)
3. Which word describes a made-up story about a roving wild dog? (4)
4. What describes the main actor in a play and a dog's leash? (4)

5. What can be doses of medication or biomass wood fuel? (7)
6. Which Victorian novelist Charles had a dog named Timber Doodle? (7)
9. Which blue-coloured cartoon hound sang 'Oh My Darling, Clementine'? (9)
14. What's the name shared between a dog food product and bread? (4)

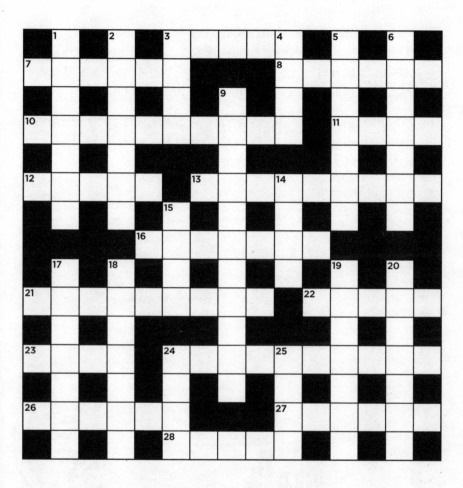

15. The saying goes that his bark is worse than his what? (4)

17. Growling and barking can be signs of stress and what else? (7)

18. Which name links what dogs are and a US sitcom set in New York? (7)

19. Which word describes Sir Edward Landseer, who worked with dogs? (7)

20. What can be a musical instrument or a call to attract a dog? (7)

24. Which word means break food down to make it easier to swallow? (4)

25. Which word means 'possesses' and is responsible for a dog? (4)

LOST DOG

Solution on page 243.

The three letters in the word DOG have been replaced by question marks in the word below. Each question mark could be a D, an O or a G. It could be only one, two or three of those letters, or it could be more than one of any as well.

The other letters of the alphabet are in place. Can you replace the question marks with D, O or G to find the word? We give you a clue to help you find what has gone missing.

? I A L ? ? U E

CLUE:
Conversation

KEEP IN SHAPE

Solution on page 244.

Individual letters have been replaced by symbols. The first group stands for the letters B, A, R, K, E and D – making the word BARKED. The symbols remain constant throughout all the groups.

What dog-related words do the other groups make?

GIVE ME FIVE!

Solution on page 244.

Solve the canine clues, which are listed at random. All the answers contain five letters. You have to fit the answers back in the frame, going either across or down.

There is a starter letter to help you on the way. There is only one way to fit all the words back.

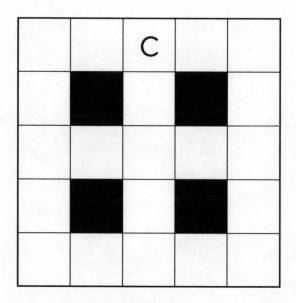

CLUES

Has a good time, frolics

Go up a tree or a hill

Open area

Light coat with black tips

Large breed originally from Japan

Organised groups of hounds

A TO Z

Solution on page 245.

Here's an A to Z of dog-related words (minus an X!). The words are hidden in the letter square. All words are in straight lines and can go horizontally, vertically and diagonally. They may read forwards or backwards.

There is one word that appears twice. Can you sniff it out?

AMBLE	JUMP	SAUNTER
BEFRIEND	KEEN	TRUSTWORTHY
CALL	LOYAL	UNDERSTAND
DASH	MOVE	VIGOROUS
ENERGY	NURTURE	WAKE
FAITHFUL	OBEDIENT	YOUNG
GENTLE	PACK	ZEST
HAPPY	QUICK	
INDIVIDUAL	RASCAL	

```
O  Z  Y  P  P  A  H  N  M  L  Q  U  C  E  D
X  B  M  E  R  O  K  U  M  O  J  I  A  R  D
L  U  E  Z  T  C  P  N  V  Y  V  E  L  O  Y
J  I  N  D  I  V  I  D  U  A  L  E  L  G  H
A  W  O  U  I  Q  U  E  L  L  T  O  R  A  T
R  U  Q  D  N  E  I  R  F  E  B  E  Z  H  R
V  Z  P  H  A  R  N  S  A  U  N  T  E  R  O
L  I  P  O  E  S  R  T  I  E  P  B  W  O  W
E  G  G  R  N  A  H  A  T  Y  O  A  M  E  T
P  E  Y  O  S  N  M  N  H  E  K  X  C  G  S
A  N  D  C  R  B  O  D  F  E  W  Y  N  K  U
S  T  A  B  L  O  K  N  U  R  T  U  R  E  R
D  L  L  E  G  E  U  J  L  Y  O  S  Q  U  T
Z  E  T  R  E  D  P  S  H  Y  E  B  E  R  D
L  U  R  N  H  L  U  F  H  T  I  A  F  Z  Y
```

POINTER

Solution on page 245.

Each answer contains FOUR letters. The first letter goes in a numbered triangle, the second letter directly above it, the third letter to the right and the fourth to the left.

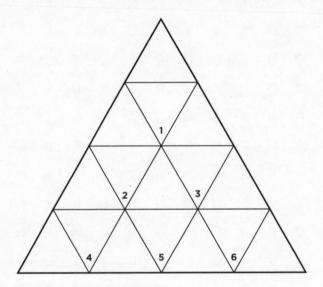

CLUES

1. Cry to frighten animals out of the way!

2. Timid character in *David Copperfield* with a dog called Jip

3. Barren tract of land used for field sports

4. She starred in a film with the Tramp

5. Brought up, nurtured

6. Treat for a dog to chew on

A TO Z

Solution on page 246.

Canine stars of TV and radio have had the letters in their names mixed up and rearranged in alphabetical order. Can you work them all out?

We give you the number of words in the name and the name of the programme to help you along.

1. A A H H O P R
   (*Downton Abbey*)

2. A A E E H I L L L N P R S S T T
   (3 words – *The Simpsons*)

3. C I I K O O R T W
   (2 words – *All Creatures Great and Small*)

4. A B I N R
   (*Family Guy*)

5. C F F R S U
   (*The Archers*)

TAKE CARE!

Solution on page 246.

We all care for our canine friends. In this puzzle you need to take care to fit the listed words into the three empty square grids to make THREE word squares which will read the same whether reading across or down.

However much care you take, there is one word that will be left out.

ACTS	CARE	REST
AREA	EATS	SEES
AWAY	EYES	TRUE
CARE	PACE	
CARE	PLAY	

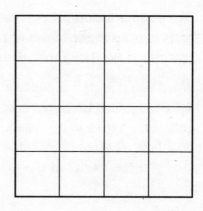

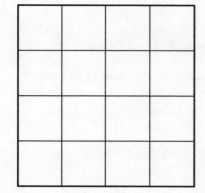

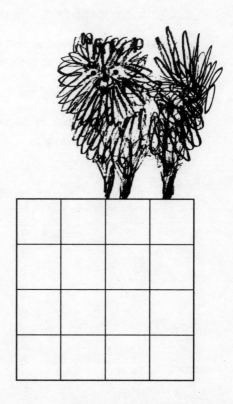

IDENTI-DOG

Solution on page 247.

Five dogs are all different breeds. They are all different ages and have a different favourite food. From the clues given, can you match each dog to their breed, age and favourite dish?

When you discover a positive piece of information that definitely links things together, put a tick in the appropriate space in the grid. Put a cross in any space where you are sure there cannot be a link. Keep re-reading the clues and adding ticks or crosses until you can work out the full solution.

CLUES

1. Jake loves biscuits

2. Chocolate is the favourite of the oldest of the five animals

3. The Peke, who loves a dish of milk, is half the age of Brandy, whose favourite food isn't meat

4. The Labrador is aged six

5. The combined ages of Suzie and Barney the Collie equals the age of the Mongrel

	BREED					AGE				FOOD				
	COLLIE	LABRADOR	MONGREL	PEKE	TERRIER	THREE	FOUR	SIX	EIGHT	ELEVEN	BISCUITS	BONES	CHOCOLATE	MEAT	MILK
NAME BARNEY															
BELLA															
BRANDY															
JAKE															
SUZIE															
FOOD BISCUITS															
BONES															
CHOCOLATE															
MEAT															
MILK															
AGE THREE															
FOUR															
SIX															
EIGHT															
ELEVEN															

K9

Solution on page 247.

A 9 x 9 crossword with a cryptic twist.

ACROSS

3. In show, the best of breed, the top of its category (5)
6. In good health at the source of water (4)
7. Unite to release an animal (5)
8. Found on a dog and a stalk of wheat (4)
10. Not able to relax, past or present (5)
14. Thank myself animal is no longer wild (4)
15. A wits concoction as the dog stays as ordered (5)
16. Meg a revealing name? That's excellent! (4)
17. Share about and picks up sounds (5)

DOWN

1. The dog's master is nothing before a confused wren (5)
2. Alter move ready and waiting (5)
4. Hens to merge in all truth (6)
5. Getting agitated, Liam the dog may chew the postman's delivery (4)
9. Canine-breed crossword compiler (6)
11. Age uncertain with regard to keenness (5)
12. Last letter moves back after a hard-run relay. Take it easy! (5)
13. Dig over an acre and look after an animal (4)

SHADY SEVENS

Solution on page 248.

Place all the listed seven-letter words to read across the grid
in such an order that the diagonal line of letters in the shaded
seven spaces forms the name of a breed of dog.

AGILITY

BISCUIT

JUMPING

MONGREL

TRAIPSE

WALKING

WHISTLE

MULTIPLE CHEWS

Solution on page 248.

Chew on these multiple choice quiz questions on the world of entertainment.

1. Ashleigh Butler won *Britain's Got Talent* in 2012 with a dog who had the same name as which bear?

   A Biffo
   B Paddington
   C Pudsey
   D Rupert

2. What was the name of the first *Blue Peter* dog, who appeared in the first show in 1962?

   A Goldie
   B Patch
   C Petra
   D Shep

3. Who presents the award-winning TV series *For the Love of Dogs*, based at Battersea and first shown in 2012?

   A Ben Fogle
   B Christopher Timothy
   C Dermot O'Leary
   D Paul O'Grady

4. What was the name of Mickey Mouse's pet dog?

A Bingo

B Drooper

c Goofy

D Pluto

5. What is the name of the vet who stars in the TV series
The Supervet?

A Noel Fitzpatrick

B Noel Kirkpatrick

c Neil Fitzpatrick

D Neil Kirkpatrick

6. In the Canadian TV series *The Littlest Hobo*, what breed
of dog is the titular Hobo?

A German shepherd

B Golden retriever

c Husky

D Labrador

7. David Bowie released a 1974 album called what type of 'Dogs'?

A Coral

B Diamond

C Emerald

D Sapphire

8. The St Bernard called Schnorbitz belonged to which 1970s entertainer?

A Bernie Winters

B Bruce Forsyth

C Des O'Connor

D Dick Emery

9. In the game of *Monopoly*, what breed of dog is one of the playing pieces?

A Cairn terrier

B Scottish terrier

C Skye terrier

D West Highland terrier

10. What was the name of the dog who appeared on HMV (His Master's Voice) record labels?

A Baxter

B Nipper

C Tucker

D Zippy

11. On their 1971 unnamed album (often referred to as *Led Zeppelin IV*), the group Led Zeppelin sang about what type of dog?

A Bad

B Black

C Good

D White

12. Lassie, whose first film was *Lassie Come Home* in 1943, was what breed of dog?

A Bearded collie

B Border collie

C Rough collie

D Smooth collie

SIXTH SENSE

Solution on page 249.

Does a dog have a sixth sense, an ability to make something out that humans are unable to? With this puzzle it's not what you see that matters, it's what you cannot see! There's a jumble of letters of the alphabet in the box.

What you need to find are the letters that do not appear. There are SIX of them. Use each missing letter once only to make the name of something that all dogs like.

Z B V C
G D H J
K L N X
U O M F
Q Y T
W

CROSS BREEDS

Solution on page 249.

The letters in SEVEN words linked to the canine world have been rearranged in alphabetical order.

Can you put the letters back in their correct order and slot them in the grid so that 4 across and the centre column reading down will spell out the names of two breeds of dog?

1. D E R S T T U

2. A A H P T W Y

3. A C C H R S T

4. E E I R R R T

5. E H I P P T W

6. A B E I J N S

7. A D E I P R S

PAPERCHASE

Solution on page 249.

There are a stack of enquiries about entering the local dog show. The secretary of the society counts them all out and then starts to read them, one by one.

He takes his first break when he has made it to an enquiry in the teens. He surveys the pile of papers read and the pile that he still has to read. By chance the two digits making up the number of the enquiry he has just read could be turned round and this new number added to the pages read would combine to make the total number of enquiries.

He carries on and then takes another break while in the twenties. The same thing occurs. The digits in the number of pages read could be reversed and the new number added to the pages read number to make the total of enquiries.

The same thing happens in the thirties and again in the forties.

The total number of enquiries is an even number.

What is it?

SIX FIX

Solution on page 249.

All answers have six letters and fit into the grid reading in a clockwise direction. We give you the starting point for the answer to Clue 1, but after that you have to work out in which hexagonal cell the answer begins.

CLUES

1. Breed of dog with tight curly hair

2. Calm, submissive

3. *Cider With Rosie* author _____ Lee who has a Gloucestershire walk named after him

4. Substance a ball or ring might be made of

5. Raised, brought up

6. Save from danger or homelessness

7. Secure metal fastening on a dog collar

8. Dog which appeared in the early days of cinema

9. Female sibling from the same litter

10. Special rewards

11. Games

12. Persons

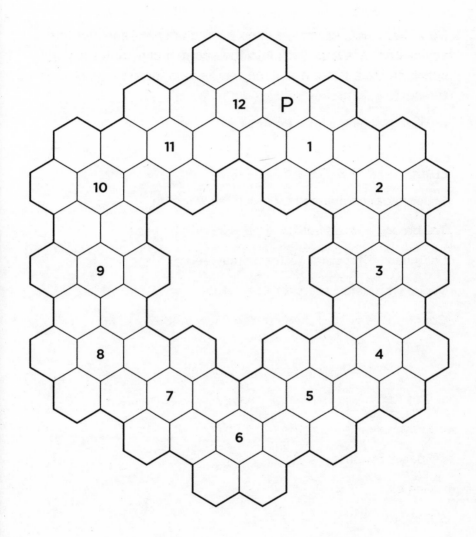

DOG COLLAR

Solution on page 250.

Solve the clues, which are in no particular order, and slot the seven-letter answers back into their correct places in the dog collar. The last letter of one answer is also the first letter of the next.

Answer 1 begins with a letter M.

CLUES

Sheer joy, accompanied by much tail wagging

Toy breed, from a Mediterranean island?

Long narrow receptacles for animal feed

Venue with tiered seats for spectators

Country that hosted the first dog show in 1859

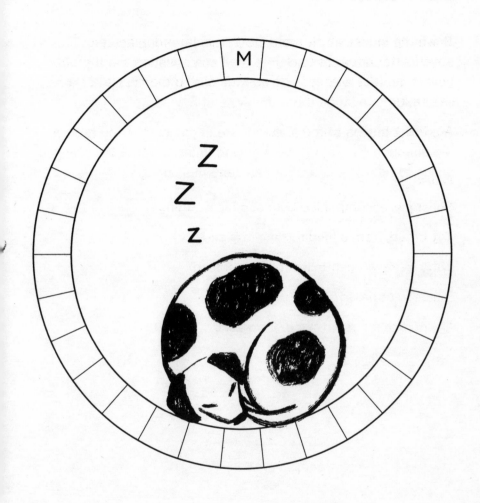

LOST DOG

Solution on page 250.

The three letters in the word DOG have been replaced by question marks in the word below. Each question mark could be a D, an O or a G. It could be only one, two or three of those letters, or it could be more than one of any as well.

The other letters of the alphabet are in place. Can you replace the question marks with D, O or G to find the word? We give you a clue to help you find what has gone missing.

? R A N ? I ? S E

CLUE:
Flamboyant

KEEP IN SHAPE

Solution on page 250.

Individual letters have been replaced by symbols. The first group stands for the letters B, E, S and T – making the word BEST.

The symbols remain constant throughout all the groups. What dog-related words do the other groups make?

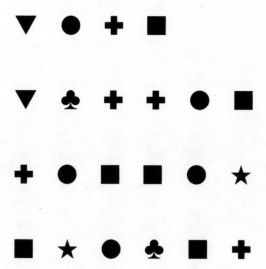

DOG TAGS

Solution on page 250.

The letters on the dog tags can be rearranged to form words. There are letters on individual tags, shared letters between two tags, and the space in the middle needs to be filled by a letter that is in all three tags.

You are looking for the names of three different breeds of gundog.

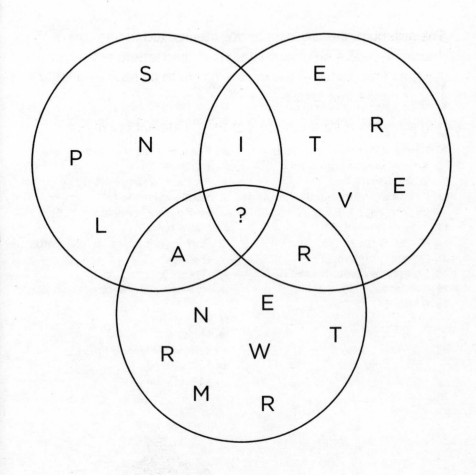

QUICK CROSSWORD

Solution on page 251.

A classic quick crossword with dog-themed clues.

ACROSS

8. Hide, used for a leash (7)
9. Open area of land (5)
10. Wash (5)
11. Hikers, with or without dogs (7)
12. A Great one maybe from Scandinavia! (4)
13. Produce moisture in the mouth prior to eating (8)
16. Type of spaniel (8)
18. Moves at speed (4)
21. Regard, approval (7)
23. Go in for a competition (5)
25. Courageous (5)
26. Amble (7)

DOWN

1. Society (4)
2. Pattern on a Skye terrier's collar? (6)
3. Farm animals rounded up by a 5 DOWN (5)
4. Increase in size, develop (4)
5. Shetland canine (7)
6. Photographic equipment (6)
7. Facial hair (8)
12. Portray, put a picture into words (8)
14. Dined (3)
15. Reacted to irritation in the nose (7)
17. Rogue (6)
19. Messy (6)
20. Take some leisure time (5)
22. Not wild (4)
24. Uncommon (4)

MULTIPLE CHEWS

Solution on page 252.

Chew on these multiple choice quiz questions based on dogs in literature.

1. In the children's book series, now a 2021 movie, what colour is Clifford, the big dog?

   A Blue
   B Green
   C Red
   D Yellow

2. Bull's-eye was the name of Bill Sikes's dog in which Charles Dickens novel?

   A *David Copperfield*
   B *Great Expectations*
   C *Nicholas Nickleby*
   D *Oliver Twist*

3. Enid Blyton's *Famous Five* novels told of the adventures of four children (Julian, Dick, Georgina – known as George – and Anne), with Georgina's dog making up the five. What was his name?

   A Sammy
   B Sonny
   C Timmy
   D Tommy

4. The dog Montmorency appears in which 1889 novel?

A *Lord of the Flies*
B *Swallows and Amazons*
C *The Wind in the Willows*
D *Three Men in a Boat*

5. In *Jane Eyre*, what is the name of Edward Rochester's dog?

A Captain
B Pilot
C Rover
D Skipper

6. The children's *Spot the Dog* book series was written by whom?

A Edward Hill
B Eric Hill
C Reginald Hill
D Rowland Hill

7. Bluebell, Jessie and Pincher are dogs who appear in which 1945 novel?

A *Animal Farm*

B *Brideshead Revisited*

C *The Catcher in the Rye*

D *To Kill a Mocking Bird*

8. What is the name of the dog who is the main protagonist in Jack London's *Call of the Wild*?

A Buck

B Chuck

C Jack

D Jake

9. In the series of children's books by New Zealand author Lynley Dodd, where is Hairy Maclary from?

A Davidson's Dairy

B Donaldson's Dairy

C Richardson's Dairy

D Robertson's Dairy

10. Jip is the dog belonging to Dora Spenlow in which Charles Dickens novel?

A *David Copperfield*

B *Great Expectations*

c *Nicholas Nickleby*

D *Oliver Twist*

11. In Enid Blyton's *Secret Seven* books, what is the name of Janet and Peter's dog?

A Scamp

B Scamper

c Skip

D Skipper

12. In the *Asterix* series of books, Dogmatix is the companion of which character?

A Asterix

B Geriatrix

c Getafix

D Obelix

DOG BASKET

Solution on page 252.

The dogs need to go in their basket. In the letter box the word DOGS appears along with three other words of four letters. The words appear in straight lines of letters that can go across, back, up, down or diagonally.

Use these words to fill the empty basket by creating a word square in which the words read the same going across and down.

R	O	G	A	L	A
W	V	W	J	W	A
E	A	B	S	X	W
Y	L	G	A	W	O
W	O	Y	R	L	W
D	W	T	Q	U	S

SHADOW PLAY

Solution on page 253.

Answer the questions going across in the top grid. All answers have seven letters, unless shown. When the top grid is complete, take the letters in the shaded squares and place them vertically, one below the other, in the lower grid.

When you have completed the lower grid, an expression about confrontation will be revealed.

CLUES

1. Making a canine sound, or the name of a London borough

2. A sign may have this followed by 'of the dog!' (six letters)

3. Take your canine companion to a kennels when you take one of these

4. Cosy woollen bed covering

5. Elongate the limbs, often after a sleep

6. Quickest, most rapid

7. Brag, draw attention to oneself (4.3)

8. Delivery person who has to be wary of dogs!

9. Call or signal by pressing the lips together

10. These dogs are often used for rounding up sheep

1							
2							
3							
4							
5							
6							
7							
8							
9							
10							

1	2	3	4	5	6	7	8	9	10

LOST DOG

Solution on page 253.

The three letters in the word DOG have been replaced by question marks in the word below. Each question mark could be a D, an O or a G. It could be only one, two or three of those letters, or it could be more than one of any as well.

The other letters of the alphabet are in place. Can you replace the question marks with D, O or G to find the word? We give you a clue to help you find what has gone missing.

? ? ? ? N E S S

CLUE:
Integrity

ABOUT BREEDING

Solution on page 253.

The names of breeds of dog have been divided into a line of letters. Can you work out the names of the two breeds in each case? Lines 1 and 2 contain two breeds of five letters; in 3 there are two seven-letter names. The letters read in chronological order.

1. A B K O I T X E A R

2. C H U A S I K R N Y

3. G R M A I F S T F O I F N F

SIRIUS

Solution on page 253.

All our dogs are stars in their own way. Sirius is known as the Dog Star and it's the brightest light in the night sky. Solve the canine clues, which are listed at random.

Each five-letter answer starts in a space with an odd number (1, 3, 5, 7, 9 and 11) and ends in a space with an even number (2, 4, 6, 8, 10 and 12).

The letter in space 1 is P.

CLUES

The thigh bone

Recreation such as racing

Smooth and shiny like a dog's coat

Lose hair

Brush and comb to look good

Young dog

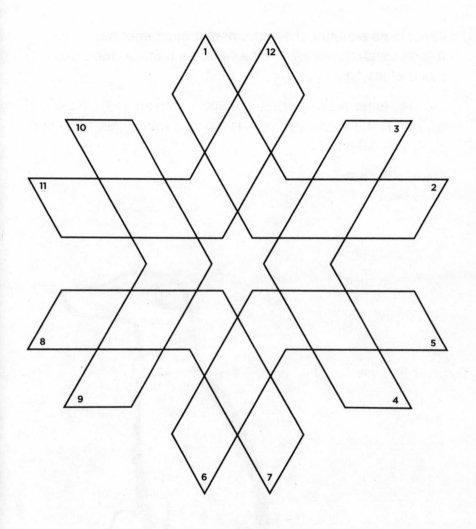

THAT'S MY DOG

Solution on page 253.

There is no doubting the breed of dog this owner has. Rearrange all the letters in the personal name to form the name of the type of dog.

M A R I E   W A R N E

CLUE:
One word

GIVE ME FIVE!

Solution on page 254.

Solve the canine clues, which are listed at random. All the answers contain five letters. You have to fit the answers back in the frame, going either across or down.

There is a starter letter to help you on the way. There is only one way to fit all the words back.

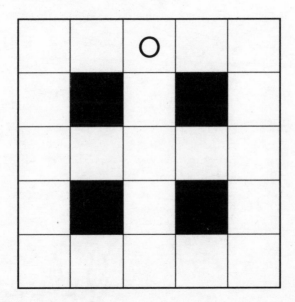

CLUES

Tugs sharply on a lead

Person who is responsible for a dog

Country roads

Homeless pet

Pet name for a pet canine

Arctic breed of working dog

KEEP IN SHAPE

Solution on page 254.

Individual letters have been replaced by symbols. The first group stands for the letters S, L, E, E and P – making the word SLEEP. The symbols remain constant throughout all the groups. What dog-related words do the other groups make?

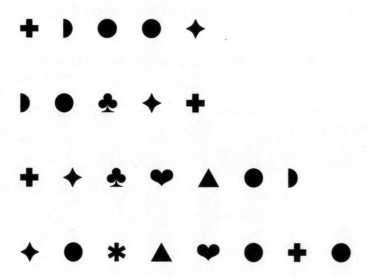

LEAD ON

Solution on page 254.

Each of the 26 letters of the alphabet has been replaced by a number from 1 to 26. Work out which number represents which letter to complete the crossword-style grid, which has words reading across and down. You are given the letters in the word LEAD to start you off. 1 = L, 2 = E, 3 = A, 4 = D. Straight away you can fill in all the squares that contain the numbers 1, 2, 3 and 4.

Fill in the 1 to 26 grid with letters of the alphabet as you work them out.

When you have worked out the code, the letters 6, 2, 25, 15, 9, 10, 6, 4, 1, 3, 6, 4, will spell out a breed of dog.

6	2	25	15	9	10	6	4	1	3	6	4

Codeword grid (each number represents a letter; black squares shown as █):

1	2	3	4	5	6	7	8	9	10	11	12	13	14	15
█	17	█	5	█	15	█	█	16	█	8	█	8	█	█
11	2	5	3	13	2	4	█	22	10	23	17	12	6	19
█	18	█	6	█	16	█	11	█	7	█	3	█	2	█
1	2	3	4	█	14	3	12	7	6	█	6	2	2	4
█	█	█	1	█	5	█	14	█	█	█	12	█	20	█
8	1	2	2	17	█	25	5	12	23	17	2	7	2	4
█	12	█	7	█	15	█	9	█	2	█	1	█	█	█
11	2	4	█	17	9	12	6	16	2	7	█	25	3	19
█	█	24	█	█	9	█	15	█	16	█	14	█	16	█
8	5	9	10	1	4	2	7	8	█	11	9	26	2	7
█	2	█	12	█	█	█	12	█	11	█	1	█	█	█
8	12	20	2	█	16	3	8	16	2	█	1	12	14	18
█	19	█	16	█	7	█	2	█	3	█	12	█	5	█
8	5	2	1	16	12	2	█	11	7	2	2	4	2	7
█	16	█	21	█	23	█	█	█	4	█	8	█	25	█

Answer key:

1	2	3	4	5	6	7	8	9	10	11	12	13

14	15	16	17	18	19	20	21	22	23	24	25	26

LOST DOG

Solution on page 255.

The three letters in the word DOG have been replaced by question marks in the word below. Each question mark could be a D, an O or a G. It could be only one, two or three of those letters, or it could be more than one of any as well.

The other letters of the alphabet are in place. Can you replace the question marks with D, O or G to find the word. We give you a clue to help you find what has gone missing.

? ? ? ? L E ?

CLUE:
Searched electronically

POINTER

Solution on page 255.

Each answer contains FOUR letters. The first letter goes in a numbered triangle, the second letter directly above it, the third letter to the right and the fourth to the left.

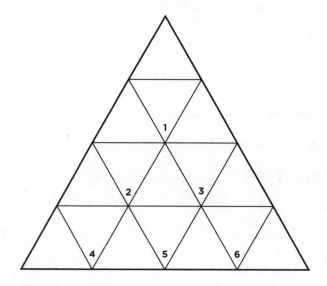

CLUES

1. It wags to show happiness

2. Sounds like a parasite but means to escape from danger

3. Male parent

4. Sleeping arrangements

5. Leather strap restraint

6. Designated space

ROUND THE BLOCK

Solution on page 255.

Many dog owners take their pet 'round the block' for a walk. In this puzzle each answer has eight letters. Write the answer words in the grid, with each first letter going in a numbered square. Then you have to decide whether to go round the block in a clockwise or anti-clockwise direction.

All the answers have to interlock together.

CLUES

1. Small dog or a French butterfly

2. Don't throw this 'toy' to a dog – it might melt!

3. Very watchful

4. The 'Bark' in *101 Dalmatians*

5. Urban footpath

6. Sleeps

7. Unfasten a collar or strap

8. Bill Sikes's dog in *Oliver!*

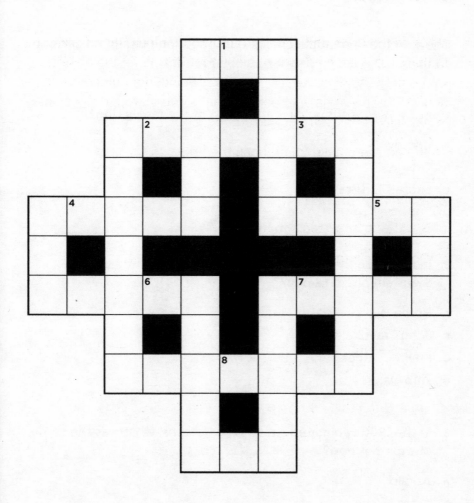

MULTIPLE CHEWS

Solution on page 256.

Chew on these multiple choice quiz questions based on cartoon canines.

1. In *The Simpsons*, what is the name of the family dog?

A Barney

B Otto

C Santa's Little Helper

D Snowball

2. In the 2008 film *Bolt*, which actor voiced the titular White Swiss shepherd puppy?

A Bruce Willis

B John Travolta

C Kevin Costner

D Tom Hanks

3. In the 1960s animated sitcom *The Jetsons*, what was the name of their pet dog?

A Apollo

B Astro

C Cosmo

D Juno

4. Scrappy-Doo is what relation to Scooby-Doo?

A Brother

B Cousin

c Nephew

D Son

5. In *Family Guy*, what is the name of the Griffin family dog?

A Bertie

B Billy

c Bobby

D Brian

6. In *Wacky Races*, Dick Dastardly and his dog Muttley raced with which number on their racing car?

A 00

B 11

c 66

D 99

7. In the *Peanuts / Charlie Brown* cartoon strips and movies, what breed of dog is Snoopy?

A Basset hound

B Beagle

c Dachshund

D Harrier

8. In Hergé's *Adventures of Tintin*, what was the name of Tintin's dog?

A Fluffy

B Frosty

c Snowy

D Sunny

9. In the 1981 film *The Fox and the Hound*, what is the name of the hound?

A Bobby

B Copper

c Goldie

D Ruby

10. What colour was the cartoon character Huckleberry Hound?

A Blue

B Green

C Red

D Yellow

11. What is the name of Peter Pan's dog?

A Dana

B Lana

C Nana

D Tina

12. What breed of dog is Scooby-Doo?

A English Mastiff

B Great Dane

C Irish Wolfhound

D Scottish Deerhound

NUMBER SUMS

Solution on page 256.

Work out the number sums with a difference below. Canine connections and mathematical know-how combine.

1. Add the number of legs in *The Famous Five* to the number of Dalmatian legs in the title of the 1996 movie.

2. Add the number of years HM Queen Elizabeth II (an owner of numerous Welsh corgis), celebrated on the throne for her Platinum Jubilee + the number of initials on the record company name that the dog 'Nipper' advertised.

3. In the latter half of the 1950s, a mongrel dog, Laika, from Moscow, travelled into outer space. If you add the exact year of Laika's journey to the number of initials in the name of her native country, what number do you get?

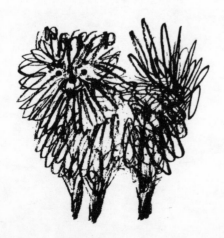

CA-NINE

Solution on page 257.

Nine boxes. Nine different letters of the alphabet. Solve the cunning clues and write the letters in the appropriate spaces in the grid.

When all nine letters are in place, a word linked to canine daily life is created.

CLUES

1. Heroic, unafraid   1   9   4   5   2

2. This word shows the dog belongs to us   7   8   9

3. Part of a dog's coat   3   4   6   9

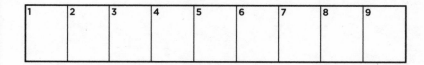

1	2	3	4	5	6	7	8	9

DOG COLLAR

Solution on page 257.

Solve the clues, which are in no particular order, and slot the seven-letter answers back into their correct places in the dog collar. The last letter of one answer is also the first letter of the next.

Answer 1 begins with a letter L.

CLUES

Walks very slowly, lags behind

Snarled

Yapping or barking shrilly

It could be Cocker or Irish Water

Devotion, fidelity

CANINE CODES

Solution on page 257.

Answer the questions across in the upper grid. All answers have eight letters. Column A reading down will reveal the name of a breed of dog. Take the key-coded letters and place them in the lower grid. For example, the first letter you need is T in square E4.

When you have finished, you will be able to complete the quotation by American humourist Robert Benchley, which begins, 'A dog teaches a boy fidelity, perseverance, and ....'

CLUES

1. Ambled around aimlessly, maybe on a walk

2. Huge, a St Bernard compared to a Yorkshire terrier, for example

3. A dog and a coastal region of Canada

4. Nationality of the clergyman who developed the Jack Russell breed

5. Regular, customary, like daily exercise

6. A living animal

7. Doing as one is told

8. Not doing as one is told, saying 'no'!

9. Brushing, combing, etc

10. A dog's name and individuality as proved by a disc or chip

	A	B	C	D	E	F	G	H
1								
2								
3								
4								
5								
6								
7								
8								
9								
10								

E4	C2		E5	F6	B9	D10					
B1	D3	D9	D8	G7	B10		D4	A5	D2	H6	C7
E10	D5	E2	E1	E8		B7	C6	C8	G3	F1	C10
H5	H10	F4	C1	H9		F3	F2	A1	G9		

BEST FOOT FORWARD

Solution on page 257.

Set off on your daily constitutional with your best friend and move forward with this puzzle. There are two clues each time and two solutions.

The first clue is general, the second has a canine link. The solutions are almost the same, the only difference being that in the second word the middle letter has moved forward in the alphabet.

1. Fruit seed * Young dog
   (both words have three letters)

2. Too self assertive * Grooming tool
   (both words have five letters)

3. Wicker containers * These dogs have long ears and short legs
   (both words have seven letters)

4. Gave orders * Praised, awarded a medal
   (both words have nine letters)

FITTING IN

Solution on page 258.

We all hope that a newcomer to the home will fit in as one of the family. In this puzzle a word with a canine connection has to be fitted in to the spaces so that the word becomes complete.

All the words in 1 need the same three-letter word, and a similar pattern follows for 2 and 3. Three different words for three different sections.

1. _ _ _ N A C E

   U N _ _ _ L E D

   _ _ _ I O U S

2. _ _ _ I O N

   C O L _ _ _ E

   P H _ _ _ M A T I C

3. C R _ _ _ E D

   B R _ _ _ I E S

   T _ _ _ N S H I P

SHADY SEVENS

Solution on page 258.

Place all the listed seven-letter words to read across the grid
in such an order that the diagonal line of letters in the shaded
seven spaces forms the name of a breed of dog.

ANGELIC   SPOTTED

FEEDING   UTILITY

SETTERS   WELFARE

SHAMPOO

1						
2						
3						
4						
5						
6						
7						

PLOTTING

Solution on page 258.

After many years of trading, a boarding kennel owner decides to call it a day. The land is square in shape, with four state-of-the-art kennels and an enclosed dog-exercising area located side by side.

The owner has four children who each have a dog. The owner wants to be very fair and make sure that each of the children gets an equal amount of land and one of the purpose-built kennel areas.

With the help of some fencing, the owner divides the plot into four areas of the same shape and size, with each area having access to a kennel.

How did he do it?

K9

Solution on page 259.

A 9 x 9 crossword with a cryptic twist.

ACROSS

3. Battersea workers's wooden stick (5)
6. Brief break, we hear, showing a dog's feet (4)
7. Spritely artificial intelligence resets leg (5)
8. Collar from the Elizabethan age sounds like a dog's bark (4)
10. Somehow I'm set recording race results (5)
14. Pedal extra hard exploring dog-walking place (4)
15. Game played on a green contains dog food (5)
16. Command the cad (4)
17. Financial fund reliance (5)

DOWN

1. Ports contain healthy games for humans and pets (5)
2. Bird describes a fast-moving dog (5)
4. Went along behind and clearly identified (6)
5. Tripped over when walking a high mountain (4)
9. Plays cricket in meadows (6)
11. Dave's arranged a rescued animal (5)
12. Marrow-bone product served at a child's party? (5)
13. A golfing cry, we hear, gives the number of legs of a dog (4)

DOG TAGS

Solution on page 259.

The letters on the dog tags can be rearranged to form words. There are letters on individual tags, shared letters between two tags, and the space in the middle needs to be filled by a letter that is in all three tags.

You are looking for the names of three locations, which give their names to different breeds of terrier.

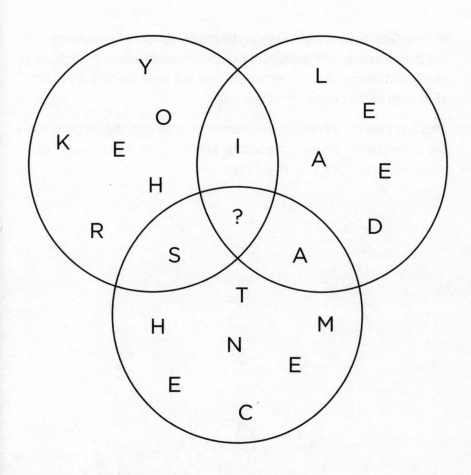

SIXTH SENSE

Solution on page 260.

Does a dog have a sixth sense, an ability to make something out that humans are unable to? With this puzzle it's not what you see that matters, it's what you cannot see! There's a jumble of letters of the alphabet in the box.

What you need to find are the letters that do not appear. There are SIX of them. Use each missing letter once only to make the name of something that most dogs like.

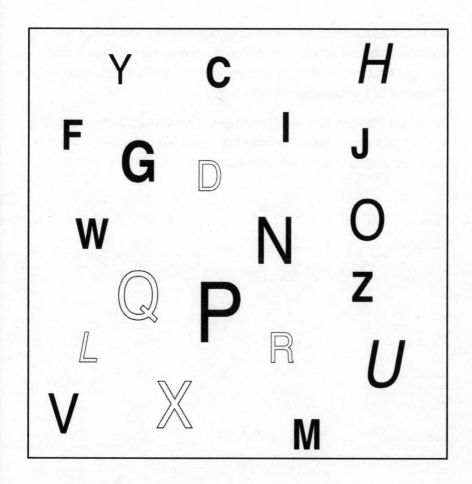

KEEP MOVING

Solution on page 260.

All the listed words are about how dogs move. The words are hidden in the letter square. All words are in straight lines and can go horizontally, vertically and diagonally. They may read forwards or backwards.

When all the words have been found, the unused letters reading left to right and top to bottom of the grid will spell out a famous canine cartoon couple who appeared in a moving adventure.

BOLT	JUMP	SCURRY
BOUNCE	LEAP	SHIFT
BOUND	LOLLOP	SPEED
CAREER	LOPE	SPRING
CHASE	MOVE	SPRINT
DART	PAD	SWIFT
DASH	RACE	TEAR
HASTEN	RUNNING	WALK
HURRY	RUSH	
JOG	SCAMPER	

```
B H A S T E N P O P Y S
R O J L O P E N A R P L
G E U U M O V E R R Y O
N S P N M G L U I R S L
I W J M C P H N R B P L
N I O R A E T U O O R O
N F G T R C C A N L I P
U T R D E S S S D T N P
R A A D E E P S H E G D
D S R D R E C A R I I A
H W A L K R U S H T F P
B O U N D A E S A H C T
```

MULTIPLE CHEWS

Solution on page 261.

Chew on these multiple choice quiz questions in a test of your general dog knowledge.

1. What is the name of the three-headed dog in Greek mythology?

   A Cerberus

   B Ceres

   C Chimaera

   D Chiron

2. What was the name of the Russian dog who was one of the first animals to go into space and was the first to orbit the Earth?

   A Laika

   B Lana

   C Layla

   D Linka

3. What was the name of the dog who found the World Cup in 1966 after it had been stolen?

   A Patches

   B Pickles

   C Pongo

   D Prince

4. What was the name of the dog who traditionally appeared in Punch and Judy shows?

A Timmy

B Toby

C Toto

D Troy

5. In the *Beano* comic, what was the name of Dennis the Menace's dog?

A Basher

B Crasher

C Dasher

D Gnasher

6. One of Orion's hunting dogs, what is the Latin name for the constellation that means 'greater dog' in English?

A Canis Major

B Canis Minor

C Ursa Major

D Ursa Minor

7. In Greek mythology, which queen of Troy was turned into a dog and threw herself into the sea?

A Cassandra
B Clytemnestra
C Hecuba
D Penelope

8. Which group of islands was named from the Latin meaning 'Island of the Dogs'?

A Azores
B Bahamas
C Balearic Islands
D Canary Islands

9. Which English poet had a Newfoundland dog called Boatswain?

A John Keats
B Lord Byron
C Percy Bysshe Shelley
D William Wordsworth

10. Chihuahuas originally come from which country in the Americas?

A Costa Rica

B Cuba

C Mexico

D Panama

11. The 'Dog Star' is the nickname for which star, the brightest in the night sky?

A Betelgeuse

B Rigel

C Sirius

D Vega

12. Corgis originate from which country in the United Kingdom?

A England

B Northern Ireland

C Scotland

D Wales

STEP-UPS

Solution on page 261.

Solve the clues, which are arranged at random, and place the answers in the frame. The shortest answer contains THREE letters, the FOUR-letter answer contains these three plus a new letter. The order can be moved around.

Keep making these step-ups until you have discovered the SEVEN-letter word, which is a breed of dog.

CLUES:

Schemes, ideas for the future

Short sleep

Breed of dog

Aircraft

They go with pots in the kitchen

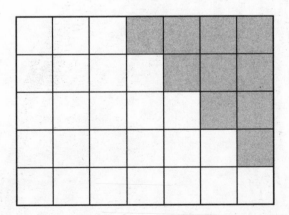

HIDE AND SEEK

Solution on page 262.

In this puzzle you must seek out popular names for dogs. The names all refer to a dog's colour and are hidden in the sentences below.

They can be found by linking words or parts of words together.

1. It is now your opportunity to become best of breed.

2. I was thinking in Geraldine's case a small dog would be better.

3. Her puppy dug up a fossil very close to this location.

4. From the centre a clear view was very visible indeed.

5. I am Berlin-bound during the middle of next week.

NUMBER SUMS

Solution on page 262.

Work out the number sums with a difference below. Canine connections and mathematical know-how combine.

1. Add the number of legs *Lady and the Tramp* possesses to the number of starring dogs in *Homeward Bound*.

2. Add the number of letters in the name of Dorothy's dog in *The Wizard of Oz* to the number of legs shared by *Turner and Hooch*.

3. Add the number of letters in the name of the movie based on Dick King Smith's *The Sheep-Pig* to the number of letters in the name of the protective Newfoundland dog in *Peter Pan*.

CROSS BREEDS

Solution on page 263.

The letters in SEVEN words linked to the canine world have been rearranged in alphabetical order.

Can you put the letters back in their correct order and slot them in the grid so that 4 across and the centre column reading down will spell out the names of two breeds of dog?

1. C E L M S S U

2. D E G M O O R

3. A E H H L T Y

4. B D G L L O U

5. A E I N R R T

6. E C H R S T T

7. A C E L S S S

WORTH IT!

Solution on page 263.

What's a dog worth? They are all beyond price, of course. However, with these dogs we have taken the letters from their names and given them each a value. Six different letters in all are used.

The numbers allocated are between 1 and 6. The total of each name is worked out by adding individual letters together.

M I A = 7

E M M A = 7

E L L A = 17

What is A L F I E worth?

CA-NINE

Solution on page 263.

Nine boxes. Nine different letters of the alphabet. Solve the cunning clues and write the letters in the appropriate spaces in the grid.

When all nine letters are in place, a word for a canine breed is created.

CLUES

1. Earth, or a sports field   1 2 6 7 8 9

2. A champion, a star   5 3 2 6

3. Puppies, or any baby animals   4 6 7 8 1

1	2	3	4	5	6	7	8	9

QUICK CROSSWORD

Solution on page 264.

A classic quick crossword with dog-themed clues.

ACROSS

8. The Alaskan Malamute hails from this continent (7)
9. Picture (5)
10. Depart (5)
11. Refined, cultivated (7)
12. A trial, in agility, for example (4)
13. The Scottish terrier also has this city's name (8)
16. Manner, demeanour (8)
18. Moves the tail from side to side (4)
21. Groups on watch (7)
23. Instruct (5)
25. A superior group (5)
26. Protected (7)

DOWN

1. Spherical plaything (4)
2. Decorations, badges (6)
3. Declined due to grief (5)
4. Identification, such as Spot or Rover (4)
5. Comes into view (7)
6. Old age (6)
7. Habits, systems (8)
12. Crushed underfoot (8)
14. Sleeping place (3)
15. Caressed (7)
17. Tasty morsel (6)
19. Prizes (6)
20. Homeless dog (5)
22. Indication (4)
24. Conceal (4)

ROUND THE BLOCK

Solution on page 264.

Many dog owners take their pet 'round the block' for a walk.
In this puzzle each answer has eight letters. Write the answer
words in the grid, with each first letter going in a numbered
square. Then you have to decide whether to go round the block
in a clockwise or anti-clockwise direction.

All the answers have to interlock together.

CLUES

1. Greyhound cross-breed dogs once associated with poaching

2. Cute and charming, like a litter of puppies

3. Describes a family pet as opposed to a working dog

4. Ball-and-socket joint

5. Those who watch a dog show

6. Wild country where sheep may graze and sheepdogs work

7. Unravel a maze of mixed-up leads

8. Education in specific skills

LOST DOG

Solution on page 265.

The three letters in the word DOG have been replaced by question marks in the word below. Each question mark could be a D, an O or a G. It could be only one, two or three of those letters, or it could be more than one of any as well.

The other letters of the alphabet are in place. Can you replace the question marks with D, O or G to find the word? We give you a clue to help you find what has gone missing.

T   H   ?   R   ?   U   ?   H   B   R   E   ?

CLUE:
Pedigree

SIXTH SENSE

Solution on page 265.

Does a dog have a sixth sense, an ability to make something out that humans are unable to? With this puzzle it's not what you see that matters, it's what you cannot see! There's a jumble of letters of the alphabet in the box.

What you need to find are the letters that do not appear. There are SIX of them. Use each missing letter once only to make a word describing a healthy, happy dog.

MULTIPLE CHEWS

Solution on page 265.

Chew on these multiple choice quiz questions based on much-loved modern films.

1. 1995: In *Toy Story*, the first computer-animated feature film, which also spawned three sequels, what was the name of the toy dachshund?

    A Dinky
    B Pinky
    c Slinky
    D Stinky

2. 1995: In *Babe*, what was the name of the female border collie who adopts the titular pig and teaches him how to herd sheep?

    A Ant
    B Bug
    c Flea
    D Fly

3. 1996: In *101 Dalmatians*, what was the name of the lead male Dalmatian?

    A Bingo
    B Bongo
    c Pogo
    D Pongo

4. 1996: In *101 Dalmatians*, what was the name of the lead female Dalmatian?

A Anita

B Juanita

C Lolita

D Perdita

5. 2000: In *How the Grinch Stole Christmas*, what was the name of the Grinch's loyal dog?

A Felix

B Lennox

C Max

D Rex

6. 2001: In *Harry Potter and the Philosopher's Stone*, what was the name of the three-headed dog based on Cerberus in Greek mythology?

A Fluffy

B Furry

C Fuzzy

D Softy

7. 2001: In *Harry Potter and the Philosopher's Stone*, what is the name of Hagrid's dog?

A Claw

B Fang

C Hook

D Tusk

8. 2001: In *Legally Blonde* and its 2003 sequel, what was the name of Reese Witherspoon's pet Chihuahua?

A Bruiser

B Brutus

C Crusher

D Tyson

9. 2007: In *I Am Legend*, what was the name of the German shepherd who was Will Smith's companion and best friend?

A Jessica / Jess

B Katrina / Kat

C Magdalena / Maggie

D Samantha / Sam

10. 2008: In *Marley and Me*, what breed of dog is Marley?

A English setter
B Golden retriever
C Irish setter
D Labrador retriever

11. 2011: In the black-and-white film *The Artist*, what is the name of the lead character's pet Jack Russell?

A Jack
B Jacko
C Jake
D Jasper

12. 2018: *Isle of Dogs* is a stop-motion film following the story of Atari Kobayashi as he attempts to find his lost dog, Spots. Which creative filmmaker wrote and directed the film?

A Quentin Tarantino
B Wes Anderson
C Steven Spielberg
D Tim Burton

DOG COLLAR

Solution on page 266.

Solve the clues, which are in no particular order, and slot the seven-letter answers back into their correct places in the dog collar. The last letter of one answer is also the first letter of the next.

Answer 1 begins with a letter H.

CLUES

Saved from danger

Breed of dog, the Dandie _____

Alleviate an itch!

In the direction of a person or place

Police-dog trainer

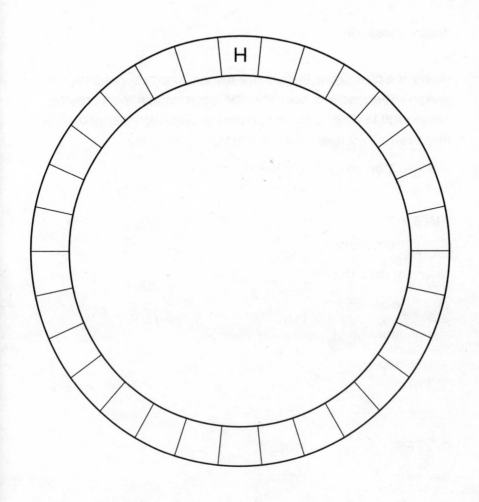

NAME GAME

Solution on page 266.

Here's a list of some of the UK's favourite dog names in recent years. The words are hidden in the letter square. All words are in straight lines and can go horizontally, vertically and diagonally. They may read forwards or backwards.

ALFIE	HOLLY	POPPY
BAILEY	HUGO	REGGIE
BARNEY	JACK	ROSIE
BETTY	LOLA	RUBY
BONNIE	LUCY	TEDDY
CHARLIE	LUNA	TOBY
CHESTER	MAX	WILLOW
DAISY	MILLIE	WINNIE
DEXTER	MOLLY	
GEORGE	OSCAR	

C	H	U	G	O	X	E	I	N	N	I	W
H	H	J	L	Y	S	I	A	D	L	I	D
E	O	A	U	M	P	V	G	R	L	T	E
S	L	L	R	N	A	P	E	L	A	E	X
T	M	O	L	L	Y	E	O	N	N	D	T
E	N	U	F	Y	I	W	R	P	U	D	E
R	C	I	T	N	M	E	G	A	L	Y	R
Y	E	T	N	D	A	S	E	A	E	T	E
Z	E	O	Y	L	X	E	I	L	L	I	M
B	B	B	R	E	G	G	I	E	S	O	Y
I	U	Y	E	N	R	A	B'	O	U	O	L
R	K	C	A	J	B	U	R	A	C	S	O

POINTER

Solution on page 267.

Each answer contains FOUR letters. The first letter goes in a numbered triangle, the second letter directly above it, the third letter to the right and the fourth to the left.

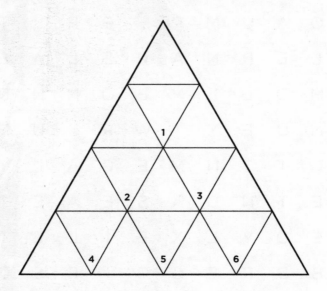

CLUES

1. Take a sly look at this abbreviation of a small dog

2. Own a dog and look after it

3. Terrier from a Scottish isle

4. Breed of Tibetan origin, Lhasa _____

5. Disorder, the result of a puppy's playfulness

6. Organs of sight

K9

Solution on page 267.

A 9 x 9 crossword with a cryptic twist.

ACROSS

3. Can you teach one of these to an old dog? (5)
6. Strangely tied to a food regime (4)
7. Waste produced from dogs' paws (5)
8. Beat with a dog's sign of affection (4)
10. This is stimulated by your pet digging earth (5)
14. Time for a twilight bark? (4)
15. Relentlessly pursue a type of dog (5)
16. Wounds starting to get better, so partly healthy (4)
17. Dogs' breakfasts? The same 50 ingredients all mixed together (5)

DOWN

1. Fully developed at endlessly dull meeting (5)
2. Go and bring back making an instant cash return (5)
4. Find a well-earned treat for your pet in an untidy drawer (6)
5. Dog's hair or a covering of paint (4)
9. In the doghouse. It's home! (6)
11. Brute of an undersoil root often dug out of the flower bed (5)
12. Don't start a task ill-equipped. Search out ability (5)
13. Type of china a dog may like? (4)

SIRIUS

Solution on page 267.

All our dogs are stars in their own way. Sirius is known as the Dog Star and it's the brightest light in the night sky. Solve the canine clues, which are listed at random.

Each five-letter answer starts in a space with an odd number (1, 3, 5, 7, 9 and 11) and ends in a space with an even number (2, 4, 6, 8, 10 and 12).

The letter in space 1 is A.

CLUES

Ascertain how heavy a dog is

Canines and molars

Leather band with a fastening

A dog needs a lot of this liquid

Nimble, active

Doze

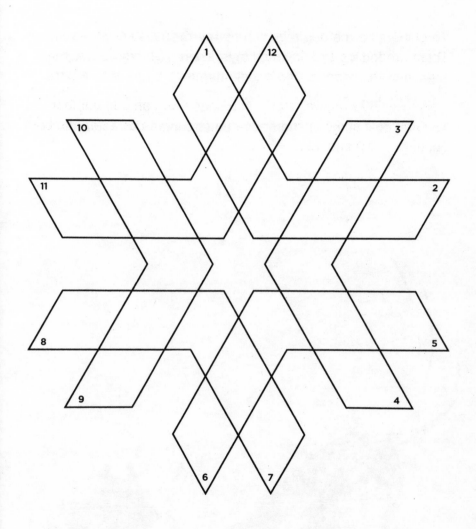

DOG TAGS

Solution on page 268.

The letters on the dog tags can be rearranged to form words. There are letters on individual tags, shared letters between two tags, and the space in the middle needs to be filled by a letter that is in all three tags.

You are looking for the names of three canine characters from fiction.

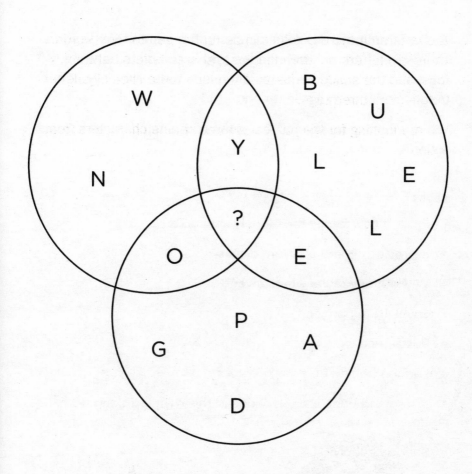

SHADOW PLAY

Solution on page 268.

Answer the questions going across in the top grid. All answers have seven letters. When the top grid is complete, take the letters in the shaded squares and place them vertically, one below the other, in the lower grid.

When you have completed the lower grid, a famous proverb with a canine connection will be revealed.

CLUES

1. Finds a new family for a lonely canine

2. It provides immunity from disease

3. Without any faults whatsoever

4. Saves from danger

5. Postponed, held up

6. Lagged behind on a walk

7. A dog and bone is a telephone in this rhyming slang from the East End

8. Snarled deeply

9. Pursuing, chasing a prey

10. Fidelity, dependability

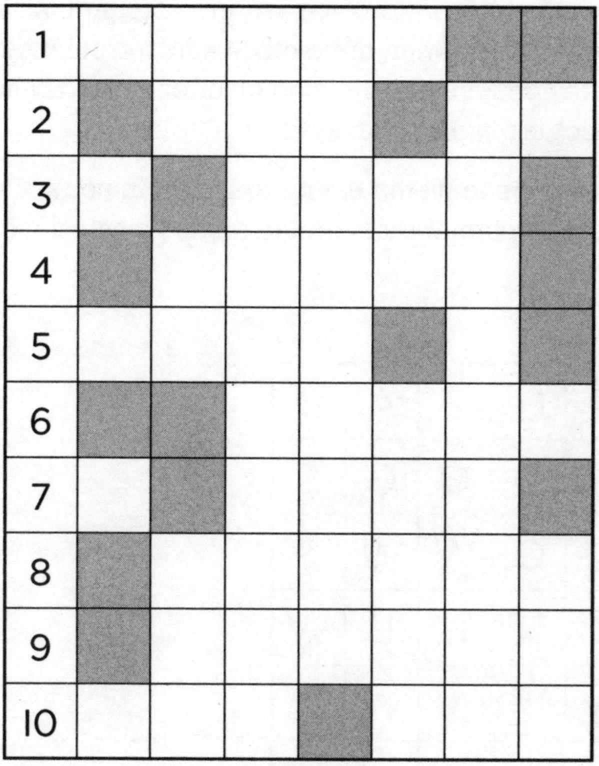

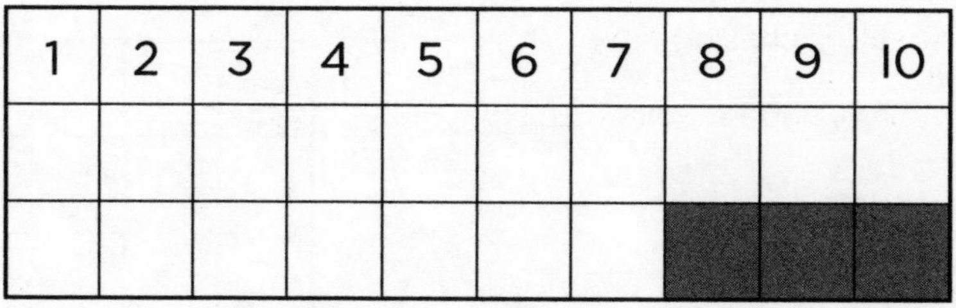

DOG BASKET

Solution on page 268.

The dogs need to go in their basket. In the letter box the word
DOGS appears along with three other words of four letters.
The words appear in straight lines of letters that can go
across, back, up, down or diagonally.

Use these words to fill the empty basket by creating a word
square in which the words read the same going across
and down.

N	Q	U	Z	A	D
Y	W	D	O	G	S
O	Q	O	W	W	S
B	U	R	G	E	W
O	W	I	N	W	R
E	Y	D	W	P	L

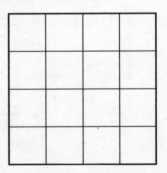

THAT'S MY DOG

Solution on page 269.

There is no doubting the breed of dog this owner has.
Rearrange all the letters in the personal name to form the
name of the type of dog.

R O B   C O R D E L L I E

CLUE:

Two words

A TO Z

Solution on page 269.

Films about canine stars of the silver screen have had the letters in their names mixed up and rearranged in alphabetical order. Can you work them all out?

We give you the number of words in the films to help you. We also give you the name of a film with a number in its title.

1. B C D D D E E F F G G H I I L O O R R T
   (5 words)

2. B E H I N O S S T W
   (3 words)

3. A B D E E G L L L L N O Y
   (2 words)

4. 2 B D E E E H N N O S T V
   (2 words)

5. B E I J N
   (1 word)

CA-NINE

Solution on page 269.

Nine boxes. Nine different letters of the alphabet. Solve the cunning clues and write the letters in the appropriate spaces in the grid.

When all nine letters are in place, a canine-linked word, describing how we might describe our best friend, is created.

CLUES

1. A special reward 8 6 9 2 8

2. Eagerness, excitement 1 9 6 3 4 5 6

3. In better physical condition 1 7 8 8 9 6

1	2	3	4	5	6	7	8	9

GIVE ME FIVE!

Solution on page 269.

Solve the canine clues, which are listed at random. All the answers contain five letters. You have to fit the answers back in the frame, going either across or down.

There is a starter letter to help you on the way. There is only one way to fit all the words back.

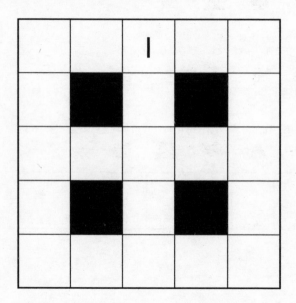

CLUES

Draw in a scent through the nose

Smooth and glossy

Remains in place

Picture

Conscious, of danger, for example

Tiny marl of a different colour, a dapple

KEEP IN SHAPE

Solution on page 270.

Individual letters have been replaced by symbols. The first group stands for the letters T, R, A, I and N – making the word TRAIN. The symbols remain constant throughout all the groups. What dog-related words do the other groups make?

QUICK CROSSWORD

Solution on page 270.

A classic quick crossword with dog-themed clues.

ACROSS

8. Give food and shelter (7)
9. Loud sounds, clamour (5)
10. Drying cloth for a wet dog! (5)
11. Breed which includes Border and Cairn (7)
12. Dish (4)
13. Search for food (8)
16. He cares for sheep (8)
18. Ground (4)
21. Dig up, find (7)
23. Rear (5)
25. Taut, secure (5)
26. Teach, train (7)

DOWN

1. Round mark on a coat (4)
2. Canine cry (3.3)
3. Meadow (5)
4. The greatest, _____ in show (4)
5. Carve a name on a name disc (7)
6. Sight (6)
7. Approach to be a chum (8)
12. Crisp treats (8)
14. A dog (3)
15. Needing a drink (7)
17. Vigour, verve (6)
19. Creature (6)
20. Class of canines (5)
22. Call to come at once (4)
24. Organs of seeing (4)

HIDE AND SEEK

Solution on page 271.

In this puzzle you must seek out the names of popular areas for dog walkers. The names are hidden in the sentences below

They can be found by linking words or parts of words together.

1. Albert's collie was a little scamp at home but well behaved at his training classes.

2. In April a new member joined the obedience group.

3. There came a downhill descent after the steep hill climb.

4. They shut railway gates in good time to protect the public.

5. They watch a favourite sitcom on Monday evenings with their pets.

MULTIPLE CHEWS

Solution on page 271.

Chew on these multiple choice quiz questions based on important dogs throughout history.

1. What was the name of US President George Washington's beloved dog?

A King Tut

B Le Beau

C Sweet Lips

D Faithful

2. Edward VII owned a Wire Fox terrier named after which leader?

A Caesar

B Napoleon

C Nero

D Wellington

3. Rufus was a famous poodle owned by which British Prime Minister?

A David Lloyd George

B Harold Wilson

C Ted Heath

D Winston Churchill

4. Martha, a Labrador mix and the dog about whom the Beatles song 'Martha My Dear' was written, belonged to which of the four Beatles?

A George Harrison

B John Lennon

c Paul McCartney

D Ringo Starr

5. Greyfriars Bobby, who became known in 19th-century Edinburgh for spending 14 years guarding his owner's grave, was what breed of dog?

A Cairn terrier

B Scottish terrier

c Skye terrier

D West Highland terrier

6. The Yorkshire terrier Mr Famous was owned by which famous American actor?

A Audrey Hepburn

B Bette Davis

c Doris Day

D Katharine Hepburn

7. Peritas was the favourite dog of which historical figure?

A Alexander the Great

B Duke of Wellington

c Julius Caesar

D Napoleon Bonaparte

8. Every dog of which breed can be traced back to 'Old Ginger', born in 1842?

A Cairn terrier

B Dandie Dinmont terrier

c Scottish terrier

D West Highland terrier

9. Charles Darwin's most famous voyage was aboard a ship with the same name as which dog?

A Barbet

B Beagle

c Boxer

D Bulldog

10. Cut and Ball were the two favourite dogs of which British monarch?

A Charles I

B Elizabeth I

c George III

D Henry VIII

11. Queen Victoria gave a Skye terrier to her mother in 1857 named after the pen name of Charles Dickens. What was it called?

A Baz

B Boz

c Raz

D Roz

12. In Homer's *The Odyssey*, what is the name of Odysseus's dog?

A Achilles

B Apollo

c Argos

D Artemis

SIX FIX

Solution on page 272.

All answers have six letters and fit into the grid reading in a clockwise direction. We give you the starting point for the answer to Clue 1, but after that you have to work out in which hexagonal cell the answer begins.

CLUES

1. Caress, smooth the dog's coat

2. Breed once known as the Russian wolfhound

3. Larger

4. Calm, kindly, like Clue 2, despite its size

5. Over indulged

6. Cup received as a prize

7. Attempt, endeavour

8. Describes soft hairy fur

9. Fully grown animals

10. Rogue, mischievous individual

11. Group of puppies born at the same time

12. Breed which might be Irish, English or Red

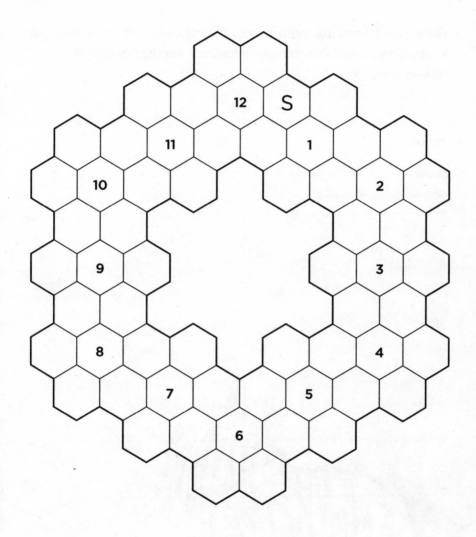

THAT'S MY DOG

Solution on page 272.

There is no doubting the breed of dog this owner has. Rearrange all the letters in the personal name to form the name of the type of dog.

TIM DALANA

CLUE:
One word

KEEP IN SHAPE

Solution on page 272.

Individual letters have been replaced by symbols. The first group stands for the letters C, O, A and T – making the word COAT. The symbols remain constant throughout all the groups. What dog-related words do the other groups make?

SIRIUS

Solution on page 272.

All our dogs are stars in their own way. Sirius is known as the Dog Star and it's the brightest light in the night sky. Solve the canine clues, which are listed at random.

Each five-letter answer starts in a space with an odd number (1, 3, 5, 7, 9 and 11) and ends in a space with an even number (2, 4, 6, 8, 10 and 12).

The letter in space 1 is C.

CLUES

Bones in the head

Type of Corgi

Talons

Offspring

Sooty's canine companion

A sled dog

CANINE CODES

Solution on page 273.

Answer the questions across in the upper grid. All answers have eight letters. Take the key-coded letters and place them in the lower grid.

To challenge you a little bit more, the words are not in order so it's up to you to rearrange them to make sense and reveal a famous proverb.

CLUES

1. Another name for a German shepherd dog

2. The overall winner at a dog show, the best!

3. Birds, but they may bear a resemblance to happy dogs

4. Discovered, as a sniffer dog might

5. A particular group at a show

6. Not inside, a place for exercise

7. The bony frame of any mammal

8. A special pseudonym for a pet or a person

9. Good looking, very fine

10. Gave a prize or treat for good work done

	A	B	C	D	E	F	G	H
1								
2								
3								
4								
5								
6								
7								
8								
9								
10								

H2	D4	C10		H5	G7	B6		B9	E8		
G2	G3	D9		E4	D1	H7	C9	E6	F4		
E1	G5	F2	C8	B7	H3		F7	H8	D10	A2	A9
H4	F6	E5									

WHAT AM I?

Solution on page 273.

Use all the clues
And give it a try,
Work out the answer,
And say what am I.

My first is in BET
But isn't in PET.

My second is in EAT
And also in VET.

My third is in TAG
And also in NAME.

My fourth's not in MEAT
But is there in GAME.

My fifth is in CALL
And also in YELP.

My sixth is in FRIEND
And also in HELP.

LOST DOG

Solution on page 273.

The three letters in the word DOG have been replaced by question marks in the word below. Each question mark could be a D, an O or a G. It could be only one, two or three of those letters, or it could be more than one of any as well.

The other letters of the alphabet are in place. Can you replace the question marks with D, O or G to find the word? We give you a clue to help you find what has gone missing.

? ? N ? ? L A

CLUE:
Sailing vessel

SOLUTIONS

KEEP IN SHAPE

LEAD

AIREDALE

REWARD

WARDEN

FAMOUS OWNERS

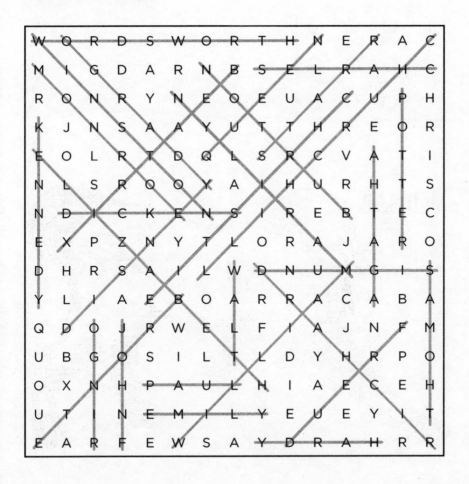

CA-NINE

1. Chase, 2. Run, 3. Sneeze.

SCHNAUZER.

DOG BASKET

G	L	A	D
L	O	G	O
A	G	O	G
D	O	G	S

MATCH UP

A / Theo / 4 / Arnold
B / Maya / 3 / Suzie
C / Lisa / 1 / Cooper
D / Alfie / 2 / Rover

WORTH IT!

MABEL is worth 20. A = 6, B = 4, E = 2, L = 3, M = 5, O = 1.

For LEO to be worth 6, the individual letters have to be 1, 2 and 3 in any order. In the name BOB, the letter B has to be more than a 3. B = 4 and O = 1 is the only possibility. The difference in the totals of BELLA and BELLE is 4 (18 – 14 = 4). B, E, L and L appear in both names, so the difference is between the E and the A. A must be the value of E plus 4. E is either a 2 or a 3. 6 is the highest of the letter values, so A must be 6 and E must be 2. In LEO the O is 1, the E is 2, so the L has to be 3. M is the only letter without a value and, as 1, 2, 3, 4 and 6 are taken, it has to be 5. MABEL is 5 + 6 + 4 + 2 + 3 = 20.

QUIZ CROSSWORD

	B		H		E	N	R	O	L		F		S
F	R	I	E	N	D				A	N	I	M	A	L
	E		A	G		S		I		C		M
T	E	A	R	J	E	R	K	E	R		T	R	O	T
	D		I			Y				I		Y
B	E	A	N	S		B	E	E	T	H	O	V	E	N
	R		G		W		T		H		N		D
			C	A	R	E	F	U	L	
	I		B		R		R		D		N		O
S	T	B	E	R	N	A	R	D		V	A	L	U	E
	A		L			I				T		T
F	L	A	G		G	R	E	Y	H	O	U	N	D	S
	I		I		A		R		O		R		O
S	A	L	U	K	I			M	E	A	D	O	W
	N		M		T	H	R	E	E		L		R

ROUND THE BLOCK

1. Exercise (C), 2. Digested (C), 3. Film star (C), 4. Passport (A),
5. American (A), 6. Lovingly (A), 7. Brittany (C), 8. Watchdog (C).

WHAT AM I?

CORGI.

The first letter is either an A or a C. The second letter is either an O or a W. The third letter is R. The fourth letter is a G or a U. The fifth letter is an I. Corgi is the only word that can be formed by the options available.

SIX-FIX

1. Beagle, 2. Garden, 3. Kennel, 4. Meekly, 5. Mature, 6. Routes, 7. Morsel, 8. Cattle, 9. Little, 10. Dawdle, 11. Wagged, 12. Begged.

SHADY SEVENS

1. Puppies,

2. Working,

3. Shih-tzu,

4. Running,

5. Stretch,

6. Spaniel,

7. Outdoor.

POINTER is formed in the shaded diagonal.

SIRIUS

1-2. Alert, 3-4. Treat, 5-6. Saint, 7-8. Snout, 9-10. Hunts, 11-12. Still.

MULTIPLE CHEWS

1. **C.** Eddie
2. **C.** Schmeichel
3. **C.** Duke
4. **B.** Buster
5. **C.** Piano
6. **B.** Roly
7. **C.** Freeway
8. **B.** Cinnamon
9. **C.** K9
10. **B.** Flash
11. **A.** Dog
12. **C.** Isis

THAT'S MY DOG

GOLDEN RETRIEVER

THREE FRIENDS

LUNA has a grey coat and is owned by Mr White.
GEORGE has a white coat and is owned by Mr Black.
WINSTON has a black coat and is owned by Ms Grey.

WALKIES

S		C		M		L		S		F		E
W	E	L	F	A	R	E		C	A	I	R	N
I		E		R		A		O		E		C
M	O	V	E	S		N	A	T	U	R	A	L
		E		H				T		C		O
C	A	R	E		L	A	Z	I	N	E	S	S
O				T		G		E				E
M	I	S	C	H	I	E	F		U	S	E	D
M		E		U			S		O			
A	T	T	E	M	P	T		C	H	U	M	S
N		T		P		I		R		G		K
D	E	L	V	E		N	A	U	G	H	T	Y
S		E		D		Y		B		T		E

DOG COLLAR

1. English, 2. Hurried, 3. Devoted, 4. Dinners, 5. Survive.

FITTING IN

1. Tag, **2.** Cur, **3.** Pet.

CROSS BREEDS

1. Command, **2.** Rewards, **3.** Eyelids, **4.** Setters, **5.** Friends, **6.** Brushed, **7.** Selects.

SETTERS and MALTESE are formed in the shaded crosses.

SIXTH SENSE

The six missing letters are D, E, F, I, N and R.
Rearranged they make the word FRIEND.

MULTIPLE CHEWS

1. **D.** Toto

2. **A.** American cocker spaniel

3. **A.** Digby

4. **A.** *Dog Day Afternoon*

5. **B.** Einstein

6. **A.** Hooch

7. **D.** Quark

8. **B.** *A Grand Day Out*

9. **B.** Beethoven

10. **C.** Golden retriever

11. **D.** Zero

12. **B.** Milo

A TO Z

Stroll appears three times.

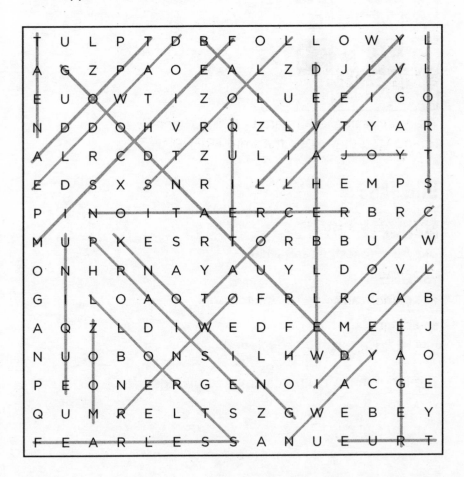

POINTER

1. Tale, 2. Meat, 3. Plea, 4. Stay, 5. Gala, 6. Heel.

GIVE ME FIVE!

DOG TAGS

TOP LEFT:
Blenheim (chestnut and white).

TOP RIGHT:
Dappled (mottle in different colours).

LOWER CIRCLE:
Flecked (light with other colours).

The letter in the centre common to all tags is an L.

WELL BRED

AFFENPINSCHER is the coded word.

1	2	3	4	5	6	7	8	9	10	11	12	13
B	R	E	D	S	T	O	N	A	I	F	G	L
14	**15**	**16**	**17**	**18**	**19**	**20**	**21**	**22**	**23**	**24**	**25**	**26**
K	Y	C	U	Q	P	M	W	H	J	V	X	Z

Words formed, reading from left to right and top to bottom of the grid:

ACROSS:
Natural, Samoyed, Bred, Likes, Pugs, Quiet, Red Setter, Pet, Rosette, Box, St Bernard, Yawns, Aged, Whelp, Move, Kennels, Utility.

DOWN:
Hair, Cuddled, Tails, Jaws, Compete, Beagle, Skye Terrier, Use, Sits, Born, Own, Feeding, Mammals, Tagged, Spitz, Walk, Vets.

SHADOW PLAY

1. Licking, 2. Guarded, 3. Stroked, 4. Sitting, 5. Charles, 6. Mongrel, 7. Feeding, 8. Pastime, 9. Weighed, 10. Hangdog.

The proverb is: 'Let sleeping dogs lie.'

THAT'S MY DOG

GREAT DANE.

BEST FOOT FORWARD

1. Vat, Vet,

2. Scant, Scent,

3. Placing, Playing,

4. Confirmed, Conformed.

SIX FIX

1. Saluki, 2. Useful, 3. Female, 4. Lapdog, 5. Golden, 6. Adored,
7. Narrow, 8. Wanted, 9. Crowds, 10. Circle, 11. Notice, 12. Vision.

ROUND THE BLOCK

1. Sealyham (C), 2. Footpath (A), 3. Doorbell (C), 4. Chestnut (A),
5. Cavalier (C), 6. Mountain (C), 7. Military (C), 8. Canadian (C).

TURN AROUND

1. Large, Regal, Elgar,
2. Ernest, Enters, Resent,
3. Grannie, Nearing, Earning.

CANINE CODES

1. Fetching, 2. Long hair, 3. Fireside, 4. Umbrella, 5. Youngest,
6. Sketched, 7. Panorama, 8. Devotion, 9. Pekinese, 10. Skywards.

The proverb reads, 'Why keep a dog and bark yourself?' This implies: why do something when there is someone else to do the job for you?

Column H reads GREAT DANES.

K9

W		T		S	H	E	E	P
H	A	I	R		O		Y	
I		M		S	W	E	E	P
T	A	I	L		L		S	
E		D	I	N	E	S		S
	L		T		D	I	S	H
T	E	E	T	H		G		O
	A		E		C	H	O	W
S	N	A	R	L		T		S

TURN AROUND

1. Dorset, Stored, Sorted,

2. Chalets, Satchel, Latches,

3. Alerting, Integral, Triangle.

ABOUT BREEDING

1. Corgi, Hound, 2. Dingo, Spitz, 3. Samoyed, Whippet.

MULTIPLE CHEWS

1. **B.** Chow Chow

2. **A.** Belgian Tervuren

3. **A.** Basenji

4. **D.** Tibet

5. **A.** Bedlington terrier

6. **B.** Devon

7. **D.** Portuguese water dog

8. **B.** Italy

9. **D.** Sir Walter Scott

10. **C.** Saluki

11. **D.** They don't have any

12. **B.** Germany

QUIZ CROSSWORD

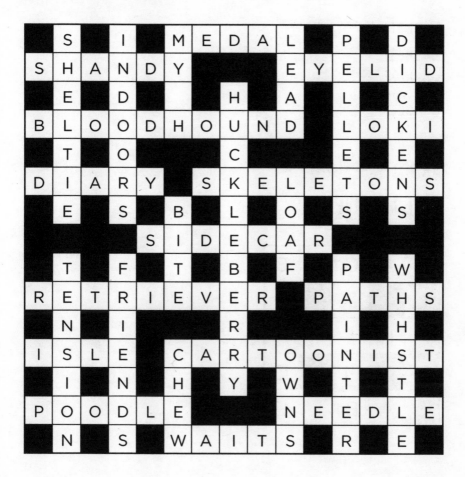

LOST DOG

Dialogue.

KEEP IN SHAPE

BARKED

BASKET

TAGGED

BEAGLE

GIVE ME FIVE!

P	A	C	K	S
L		L		P
A	K	I	T	A
Y		M		C
S	A	B	L	E

A TO Z

FAITHFUL appears twice.

POINTER

1. Shoo, 2. Dora, 3. Moor, 4. Lady, 5. Bred, 6. Bone.

A TO Z

1. Pharaoh, 2. Santa's Little Helper, 3. Tricki Woo, 4. Brian, 5. Scruff.

TAKE CARE!

The word PLAY will not fit into a word square.

C	A	R	E
A	R	E	A
R	E	S	T
E	A	T	S

A	C	T	S
C	A	R	E
T	R	U	E
S	E	E	S

P	A	C	E
A	W	A	Y
C	A	R	E
E	Y	E	S

IDENTI-DOG

BARNEY – Collie – Eight – Meat.

BELLA – Mongrel – Eleven – Chocolate.

BRANDY – Labrador – Six – Bones.

JAKE – Terrier – Four – Biscuits.

SUZIE – Peke – Three – Milk.

K9

O		A		C	H	A	M	P
W	E	L	L		O		A	
N		E		U	N	T	I	E
E	A	R	S		E		L	
R		T	E	N	S	E		R
	C		T		T	A	M	E
W	A	I	T	S		G		L
	R		E		M	E	G	A
H	E	A	R	S		R		X

SHADY SEVENS

1. Walking, 2. Whistle, 3. Agility, 4. Jumping, 5. Traipse, 6. Mongrel, 7. Biscuit.

WHIPPET is formed in the shaded diagonal.

MULTIPLE CHEWS

1. **c.** Pudsey

2. **c.** Petra

3. **d.** Paul O'Grady

4. **d.** Pluto

5. **a.** Noel Fitzpatrick

6. **a.** German shepherd

7. **b.** Diamond

8. **a.** Bernie Winters

9. **b.** Scottish terrier

10. **b.** Nipper

11. **b.** Black

12. **c.** Rough collie

SIXTH SENSE

The six missing letters are A, E, I, P, R and S. Rearranged they make the word PRAISE.

CROSS BREEDS

1. Trusted, 2. Pathway, 3. Scratch, 4. Terrier, 5. Whippet, 6. Basenji, 7. Praised.

TERRIER and SHAR-PEI are formed in the shaded crosses.

PAPERCHASE

110. The secretary first stops with 19 read and 91 to go. He then stops with 28 read and 82 to go. He stops again with 37 read and 73 to go and also stops with 46 read and 64 to go.

SIX FIX

1. Poodle, 2. Docile, 3. Laurie, 4. Rubber, 5. Reared, 6. Rescue, 7. Buckle, 8. Lassie, 9. Sister, 10. Treats, 11. Sports, 12. People.

DOG COLLAR

1. Maltese, 2. England, 3. Delight, 4. Troughs, 5. Stadium.

LOST DOG

Grandiose.

KEEP IN SHAPE

BEST
BASSET
SETTER
TREATS

DOG TAGS

TOP LEFT: Spaniel.

TOP RIGHT: Retriever.

LOWER CIRCLE: Weimaraner.

The letter in the centre common to all tags is an E.

QUICK CROSSWORD

C		T		S		G		S		C		W
L	E	A	T	H	E	R		H	E	A	T	H
U		R		E		O		E		M		I
B	A	T	H	E		W	A	L	K	E	R	S
		A		P			T		R		K
D	A	N	E		S	A	L	I	V	A	T	E
E				S		T		E			R
S	P	R	I	N	G	E	R		R	U	N	S
C		A		E			R		N		
R	E	S	P	E	C	T		E	N	T	E	R
I		C		Z		A		L		I		A
B	R	A	V	E		M	E	A	N	D	E	R
E		L		D		E		X		Y		E

MULTIPLE CHEWS

1. **c.** Red

2. **D.** *Oliver Twist*

3. **c.** Timmy

4. **D.** *Three Men in a Boat*

5. **B.** Pilot

6. **B.** Eric Hill

7. **A.** *Animal Farm*

8. **A.** Buck

9. **B.** Donaldson's Dairy

10. **A.** *David Copperfield*

11. **B.** Scamper

12. **D.** Obelix

DOG BASKET

D	O	G	S
O	V	A	L
G	A	L	A
S	L	A	B

SHADOW PLAY

1. Barking, 2. Beware, 3. Holiday, 4. Blanket, 5. Stretch, 6. Fastest, 7. Show off, 8. Postman, 9. Whistle, 10. Collies.

The expression is: 'A bone to pick with someone,' as two dogs might confront each other.

LOST DOG

Goodness.

ABOUT BREEDING

1. Akita, Boxer, 2. Cairn, Husky, 3. Griffon, Mastiff.

SIRIUS

1-2. Puppy, 3-4. Sport, 5-6. Groom, 7-8. Moult, 9-10. Sleek, 11-12. Femur.

THAT'S MY DOG

WEIMARANER.

GIVE ME FIVE!

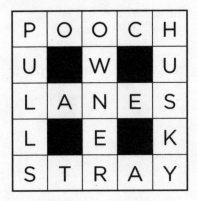

P	O	O	C	H
U	■	W	■	U
L	A	N	E	S
L	■	E	■	K
S	T	R	A	Y

KEEP IN SHAPE

SLEEP

LEAPS

SPANIEL

PEKINESE

LEAD ON

NEWFOUNDLAND is the coded word.

1	2	3	4	5	6	7	8	9	10	11	12	13
L	E	A	D	H	N	R	S	O	U	B	I	V
14	15	16	17	18	19	20	21	22	23	24	25	26
C	F	T	P	K	G	Z	Y	J	M	Q	W	X

Words formed, reading from left to right and top to bottom of the grid:

ACROSS:
Behaved, Jumping, Lead, Cairn, Need, Sleep, Whimpered, Bed, Pointer, Wag, Shoulders, Boxer, Size, Taste, Lick, Sheltie, Breeder.

DOWN:
Peke, Handler, Fetch, Turn, Spaniel, Sneeze, Bichon Frise, Lie, Meet, Food, Ate, Quietly, Collies, Height, Beard, Trim, Chew.

LOST DOG

Googled.

POINTER

1. Tail, 2. Flee, 3. Sire, 4. Beds, 5. Lead, 6. Area.

ROUND THE BLOCK

1. Papillon (C), 2. Snowball (A), 3. Vigilant (A), 4. Twilight (C), 5. Pavement (A), 6. Slumbers (A), 7. Unbuckle (A), 8. Bull's-eye (C).

MULTIPLE CHEWS

1. **c.** Santa's Little Helper

2. **B.** John Travolta

3. **B.** Astro

4. **c.** Nephew

5. **D.** Brian

6. **A.** 00

7. **B.** Beagle

8. **c.** Snowy

9. **B.** Copper

10. **A.** Blue

11. **c.** Nana

12. **B.** Great Dane

NUMBER SUMS

1. 416.
   12 legs in *The Famous Five* (4 children and a dog)
   + 404 legs in *101 Dalmatians*.

2. 73.
   Her Majesty celebrated 70 years on the throne in 2022
   and Nipper advertised HMV, which has 3 initials.

3. 1961.
   Laika, the first canine space traveller, made her journey
   in 1957 and she was from the USSR, which has 4 initials.

CA-NINE

1. Brave, 2. Our, 3. Hair.

BEHAVIOUR

DOG COLLAR

1. Loyalty, 2. Yelping, 3. Growled, 4. Dawdles, 5. Spaniel.

CANINE CODES

1. Wandered, 2. Enormous, 3. Labrador, 4. Scottish, 5. Habitual, 6. Creature, 7. Obedient, 8. Refusing, 9. Grooming, 10. Identity.

The quotation reads, 'A dog teaches a boy fidelity, perseverance, and TO TURN AROUND THREE TIMES BEFORE LYING DOWN.'

Column A makes the breed WELSH CORGI.

BEST FOOT FORWARD

1. Pip, Pup,

2. Brash, Brush,

3. Baskets, Bassets,

4. Commanded, Commended.

FITTING IN

1. Fur, 2. Leg, 3. Own.

SHADY SEVENS

1. Setters, 2. Shampoo, 3. Feeding, 4. Utility, 5. Spotted, 6. Angelic, 7. Welfare.

SHELTIE is formed in the shaded diagonal.

PLOTTING

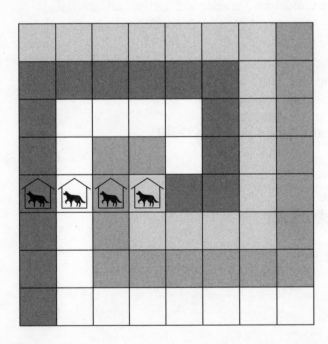

K9

S		S		S	T	A	F	F
P	A	W	S		A		E	
O		I		A	G	I	L	E
R	U	F	F		G		L	
T		T	I	M	E	S		J
	F		E		D	A	L	E
B	O	W	L	S		V		L
	U		D		H	E	E	L
T	R	U	S	T		D		Y

DOG TAGS

TOP LEFT: Yorkshire.

TOP RIGHT: Airedale.

LOWER CIRCLE: Manchester.

The letter in the centre common to all tags is an R.

SIXTH SENSE

The six missing letters are A, B, E, K, S and T.
Rearranged they make the word BASKET.

KEEP MOVING

The unused letters spell out PONGO AND PERDITA
from *101 Dalmatians*.

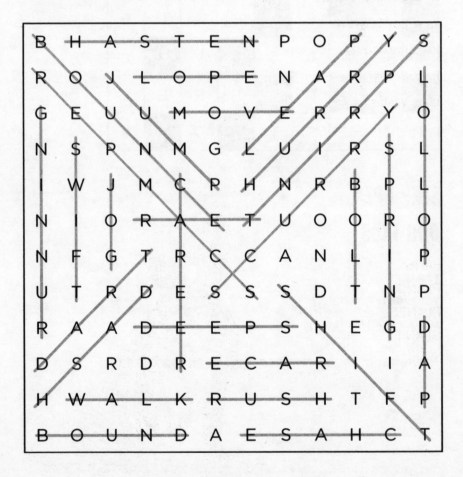

MULTIPLE CHEWS

1. **A.** Cerberus
2. **A.** Laika
3. **B.** Pickles
4. **B.** Toby
5. **D.** Gnasher
6. **A.** Canis Major
7. **C.** Hecuba
8. **D.** Canary Islands
9. **B.** Lord Byron
10. **C.** Mexico
11. **C.** Sirius
12. **D.** Wales

STEP-UPS

NAP
PANS
PLANS
PLANES
SPANIEL

HIDE AND SEEK

1. Snowy, 2. Ginger, 3. Silver, 4. Treacle, 5. Amber.

1. SNOWY. It iS NOW your opportunity to become best of breed.
2. GINGER. I was thinkinG IN GERaldine's case a small dog would be better.
3. SILVER. Her puppy dug up a fosSIL VERy close to this location.
4. TREACLE. From the cenTRE A CLEar view was very visible indeed.
5. AMBER. I AM BERlin bound during the middle of next week.

NUMBER SUMS

1. 10.
   8 legs in *Lady and the Tramp* + 2 dogs in *Homeward Bound*.

2. 10.
   Dorothy's dog is Toto and Turner and Hooch are a man and a dog.

3. 8.
   The *Sheep-Pig* became *Babe*, and Nana was the dog in *Peter Pan*.

CROSS BREEDS

1. Muscles, 2. Groomed, 3. Healthy, 4. Bulldog, 5. Trainer, 6. Stretch, 7. Classes.

BULLDOG and COLLIES are formed in the shaded crosses.

WORTH IT!

ALFIE is worth 20. A = 2, E = 3, F = 5, I = 4, L = 6, M = 1.

For MIA to be worth 7, the individual letters have to be 1, 2 and 4 in any order. In the name EMMA, the letter E cannot be a 1, 2 or 4 and has to be a 3. As the name totals 7, then A + M + M = 4. M has to be 1 and A is 2. Both EMMA and ELLA contain an E and an A. The total of ELLA is 10 greater than EMMA, which means L has to be 6. The letter F appears for the first time in ALFIE. All other values are accounted for, so F must be 5.

CA-NINE

1. Ground, 2. Hero, 3. Young.

GREYHOUND

QUICK CROSSWORD

B		M		P		N		A		D		R
A	M	E	R	I	C	A		P	H	O	T	O
L		D		N		M		P		T		U
L	E	A	V	E		E	L	E	G	A	N	T
		L		D			A		G			I
T	E	S	T		A	B	E	R	D	E	E	N
R				S		E		S				E
A	T	T	I	T	U	D	E		W	A	G	S
M		I		R			S		W			
P	A	T	R	O	L	S		T	E	A	C	H
L		B		K		I		R		R		I
E	L	I	T	E		G	U	A	R	D	E	D
D		T		D		N		Y		S		E

AROUND THE BLOCK

1. Lurchers (C), 2. Adorable (A), 3. Domestic (C), 4. Shoulder (A), 5. Audience (C), 6. Moorland (C), 7. Untangle (C), 8. Training (A).

LOST DOG

Thoroughbred.

SIXTH SENSE

The six missing letters are A, C, E, I, T and V.
Rearranged they make the word ACTIVE.

MULTIPLE CHEWS

1. **c.** Slinky
2. **D.** Fly
3. **D.** Pongo
4. **D.** Perdita
5. **c.** Max
6. **A.** Fluffy
7. **B.** Fang
8. **A.** Bruiser
9. **D.** Samantha / Sam
10. **D.** Labrador retriever
11. **A.** Jack
12. **B.** Wes Anderson

DOG COLLAR

1. Handler, **2.** Rescued, **3.** Dinmont, **4.** Towards, **5.** Scratch.

NAME GAME

POINTER

1. Peke, 2. Keep, 3. Skye, 4. Apso, 5. Mess, 6. Eyes.

K9

A	■	F	■	T	R	I	C	K
D	I	E	T	■	E	■	O	■
U	■	T	■	S	W	E	A	T
L	I	C	K	■	A	■	T	■
T	■	H	E	A	R	T	■	S
■	B	■	N	■	D	U	S	K
H	O	U	N	D	■	B	■	I
■	N	E	■	H	E	A	L	L
M	E	A	L	S	■	R	■	L

SIRIUS

1-2. Agile, 3-4. Sleep, 5-6. Teeth, 7-8. Strap, 9-10. Water, 11-12. Weigh.

DOG TAGS

TOP LEFT: Snowy (Tintin).

TOP RIGHT: Bull's-eye (*Oliver Twist*).

LOWER CIRCLE: Gaspode (Discworld).

The letter in the centre common to all tags is an S.

SHADOW PLAY

1. Rehomes, 2. Vaccine, 3. Perfect, 4. Rescues, 5. Delayed, 6. Dawdled, 7. Cockney, 8. Growled, 9. Hunting, 10. Loyalty.

The proverb is: 'Every dog has its day.'

DOG BASKET

D	O	G	S
O	B	O	E
G	O	W	N
S	E	N	D

THAT'S MY DOG

BORDER COLLIE

A TO Z

1. *Clifford the Big Red Dog*, 2. Best in Show, 3. *Legally Blonde*,
4. Beethoven's 2nd, 5. Benji.

CA-NINE

1. Treat, 2. Fervour, 3. Fitter.

FAVOURITE

GIVE ME FIVE!

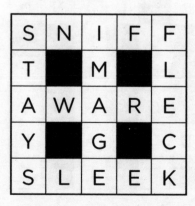

KEEP IN SHAPE

TRAIN
TERRIER
POINTER
ROUTINE

QUICK CROSSWORD

S		B		F		B		E		V		B
P	R	O	V	I	D	E		N	O	I	S	E
O		W		E		S		G		S		F
T	O	W	E	L		T	E	R	R	I	E	R
		O		D				A		O		I
B	O	W	L		S	C	A	V	E	N	G	E
I				T		U		E				N
S	H	E	P	H	E	R	D		L	A	N	D
C		N		I				G		N		
U	N	E	A	R	T	H		R	A	I	S	E
I		R		S		E		O		M		Y
T	I	G	H	T		E	D	U	C	A	T	E
S		Y		Y		L		P		L		S

HIDE AND SEEK

1. **PATH.** Albert's collie was a little scamP AT Home but well behaved at his training classes.
2. **LANE.** In ApriL A NEw member joined the obedience group.
3. **MEADOW.** There caME A DOWnhill descent after the steep hill climb.
4. **TRAIL.** They shuT RAILway gates in good time to protect the public.
5. **COMMON.** They watch a favourite sitCOM MONday evenings with their pets.

MULTIPLE CHEWS

1. **c.** Sweet Lips
2. **A.** Caesar
3. **D.** Winston Churchill
4. **c.** Paul McCartney
5. **c.** Skye terrier
6. **A.** Audrey Hepburn
7. **A.** Alexander the Great
8. **B.** Dandie Dinmont terrier
9. **B.** Beagle
10. **D.** Henry VIII
11. **B.** Boz
12. **c.** Argos

SIX FIX

1. Stroke, 2. Borzoi, 3. Bigger, 4. Gentle, 5. Spoilt, 6. Trophy, 7. Effort, 8. Fluffy, 9. Adults, 10. Rascal, 11. Litter, 12. Setter.

THAT'S MY DOG

DALMATIAN

KEEP IN SHAPE

COAT
COLLAR
TRAIL
COLLIE.

SIRIUS

1-2. Claws, 3-4. Sweep, 5-6. Welsh, 7-8. Issue, 9-10. Husky, 11-12. Skull.

CANINE CODES

1. Alsatian, 2. Champion, 3. Wagtails, 4. Detected, 5. Category,
6. Outdoors, 7. Skeleton, 8. Nickname, 9. Handsome, 10. Rewarded.

The words in order read NEW, YOU, AN, OLD, CANNOT, TRICKS,
TEACH, DOG. Rearranged, the proverb reads, 'You cannot
teach an old dog new tricks.'

WHAT AM I?

BEAGLE

The first letter is a B. The second letter is either an E or a T.
The third letter is an A. The fourth letter is a G. The fifth letter
is an L. The sixth letter is an E. Beagle is the only word that
can be formed by the options available.

LOST DOG

Gondola.

NOTES

NOTES

NOTES

NOTES

NOTES

NOTES

ALSO AVAILABLE

BATTERSEA CAT PUZZLE BOOK

ISBN 978 1 80279 413 7